A *Wild* CONSTRAINT

A *Wild* CONSTRAINT

THE CASE FOR CHASTITY

JENNY TAYLOR

continuum

Continuum International Publishing Group

The Tower Building   80 Maiden Lane
11 York Road   Suite 704
London   New York
SE1 7NX   NY 10038

www.continuumbooks.com

First published 2008

British Library Cataloguing-in-Publication Data
A catalogue record for this book is available from the British Library.

ISBN 9780826487124

Typeset by Newgen Imaging Systems Pvt Ltd, Chennai, India
Printed and bound by MPG Books, Cornwall, UK

Christ will be honoured in my body.

Philippians 1.20

Contents

Acknowledgements

This book could not have been written unless inspired by women – and some men – who practised a winsome chastity in pursuit of a selfless goal. I owe the greatest debt to the women of Interserve – the former Bible and Medical Missionary Fellowship – who modelled a completely creative life that allowed so much room for me. They had thrown themselves into projects in remote and difficult locations where men supported them as brothers, confidants and equals. The freedom, respect and dignity their self-discipline and sacrifice earned for them still informs a fellowship of unparalleled strength of purpose. I salute in particular Dr Pam Dodson, one of Nepal's first female surgeons, who gave me a home by the sea for some of the writing. She set off for the Himalayas just after the country opened, knowing the likelihood of marriage was minimal. She and those like her embraced 'the wildness of God' in a constraining idealism for which they no doubt suffered more than I can know, but which gave hope to many.

Thanks to my gentle editor Carolyn Armitage without whose quiet insistence this book would not have happened. Other debts are owed to Ida and David Coffey who provided me with an odd little cottage in the shadow of the Murrayfield Stadium in Edinburgh for six weeks without charge, while I undertook some of the research. Graham Claydon, Michael Schluter, Paul Cheverton, Elaine Storkey, Jay Smith, Jane Hawes and Carmen Schultz have all made helpful comments on the manuscript and supported me in untold ways.

I must particularly thank all those who trusted me with their stories. Thank you for your courage, friendship and example.

Introduction

My old boyfriends will no doubt hoot and jeer when they discover I'm writing a book about chastity. Of course it provokes mirth and scepticism – and curiosity. Such a quaint notion. Ever since I became a Christian two decades ago, in part through the writings of St Paul on the body, I have found myself responding, albeit reluctantly, to requests particularly from the secular media to talk about why I turned my back on sex. I am not embarrassed to do so in public if it will encourage others.

The book came about as the result of an invitation to develop an article I had published in *Third Way* magazine.[1] *The Daily Telegraph Review* had published a piece by Catherine von Ruhland about her intention, aged 40, to renounce her virginity to which I had responded robustly.[2] Catherine's piece went around the globe and was followed up by TV appearances, and then a BBC *Woman's Hour* interview with both of us. I talked about how the degradation of the personality can start innocently enough with one's first unsanctioned sexual encounter, and end in dark and increasingly wretched places. What is lost in terms of trust, self-esteem and integrity and the knock-on effects on the family and wider world is profound.

Once I began research for the book, I became aware of a curious phenomenon: there is almost nothing written for any market, be it sacred or secular, about the emotional and social costs of sexual licence. Rarely is a connection ever overtly made

---

1 'A Wild Constraint', *Third Way*, Summer 2004, 27:6, 12–13.
2 This story is related in 'An Unchosen Chastity', *Third Way*, Spring 2004, 27:5, 12–15.

between the 'healthy sex' that sells cars, holidays and just about anything else, and the sex that ends in teen pregnancies, child custody battles and a destructive binge drinking culture. That would be to stray into the realm of morality. You can moralize about smoking, smacking and fox hunting, but not something as significant as sex which affects the core of our identities and is the locus of what Alan Bloom calls 'the soul's energy'. Emotionally unprotected sex needs a health warning of its own. The horrifying reality of sexual pain and its social cost is quite simply not discussed – beyond the dismal recitation of statistics that show the true fall-out of the sexual revolution.

On the other hand, in one bookshop, there were shelves groaning with well-written, passionate volumes of opinion and advice that indicated almost panic about the very real *religious* crisis that confronts the West's sexuality. As the church re-evaluates its traditional stance on chastity and homosexuality, evangelical Christians particularly in America are deeply concerned about how to save their children from a sexually profligate culture around them. In January 2005, I counted 15 American titles published within the last two years alone with titles like *Why Women Lose when they Give In* and *Every Woman's Battle*. The books were loud, righteous and directive – but none of them talked about sex in terms of social responsibility. The British contribution, though less strident – the tone being 'we've all failed, but there could be an alternative' – was nonetheless also carried on in a vaccuum, as if individuals had sex lives, but society did not.

What struck me also was that, barring Kristin Aune's interesting piece of research, *Single Women: Challenge to the Church?*, no book looked at sexual abstinence as a coherent stance on its own terms; as a sociological phenomenon unconnected with marriage. 'Singleness' for unvowed Christians classically implies sexual abstinence – but only until marriage. It has come to have meaning only by reference to 'un-singleness'. The Silver Ring Thing had hit

Britain as a clarion call for young people to 'wait'. Chapter 8 of
J. John's book on sex is actually called 'Single and Waiting'![3]

I wanted to write a book about 'single and not waiting' – or
'living fully as if I might never have sex'; I wanted to advocate a
viable way of living that is an important social option, not a nega-
tion of something considered better but out of reach. I wanted to
write it for thinking people, whether Christian or not, who find
themselves completely bamboozled by the media; by pressure
to be sexy, have sex, have it all, and are uneasy about it. I wanted to
offer something to parents who watch anxious and bemused as
their children get sucked into the sexual rapids. And I wanted to
help single people to be an encouragement rather than a wretched
warning.

Self-knowledge is imperative in the day-by-day business of
remaining sane and honest in one's living, and one must give an
account that accommodates the sceptics. Sexuality is never without issues – and psychotherapists get fat on them. As a wild child
who ran to religion I will no doubt be criticized by both sides
in the battle for truth. I learned wisdom only through experience.
I wish it had been otherwise. It is only because I know what I lost
and what by the grace of God has been restored to me that
I agreed to write this book. The biblical guidance on sex pulled me
through a dark time – and if it is good enough to save one's life, it
is good enough to go on living by.

Care of our sexuality has traditionally been hedged about by
taboos. Everyone is unpredictably susceptible to the power and
intensity that sexual activity unleashes within them. No amount of
sociological and psychological revisionism will change that fact.
My conversations with women and men of all ages and backgrounds – for which I am profoundly in their debt – showed me

---

3   J. John, *It's Always on my Mind* (Eastbourne: Kingsway 1996).

that there is a world of pain caused by capitulation to cultural mores. I wanted to show that such pain has a more than personal cost; and that redeemed and used, there is more to sexless single-dom than mere endurance. It is not merely an absence of partner-ship, but can become a life-saving presence of freedom, order and sanity; and more than that – a source of strength for society at large. I long for this to be affirmed and modelled attractively so that young women do not waste so much of their lives capitulat-ing to men, waiting to capitulate or regretting that they did! So often they marry, and spend the rest of their lives regretting that too – or waiting for something else: a child that never comes; a bigger house, more freedom for creativity – or even for their oppressive spouse to die.

But there is more to chastity than just sexual abstinence. It is the opposite of the old credit card slogan: 'Access takes the waiting out of wanting.' The 'grab it now' culture is a direct attack on chastity. Chastity properly understood is an attitude that antic-ipates grace; that accepts there is a time and a place for all things. Learning how to wait well is the secret of maturity and satis-faction, even if it is for a lifetime. In Ronald Rolheiser's words: 'Irreverance or prematurity are what violate chastity.' By that token marrying because it promises compensation is unchaste. When it assures us of security, status and sex – and most likely a rest from the burden of ourselves – it is unchaste. Yet we opt for it because the alternative as it has been presented, seems so awful. Without outspoken advocates for chastity, women will only go on trying harder to numb themselves to the pain of emotionally unprotected sex. And all that results in is a hardening of the heart and a greater insensitivity to what really matters for society as a whole. Chastity is deeply political.

I have also been intrigued to understand what lies behind the changed attitudes of a country once a byword for reticence about sex, from where chaste women led the world in sexual and social reform. What is the link between chastity and creativity? My own experience led me to want to know more about pioneers like Florence Nightingale and Jane Austen who responded with their bodies to the needs and constraints of their time. They chose something other than marriage – and it surely was not lack of interest in men.[4]

I had inspiring role models among the missionary spinsters I'd worked with who spent decades in hard places in India and Nepal and Africa, often on their own, founding healthcare and educational opportunities especially for other women. Ordinary, unmarried and chaste, they often achieved something beautiful for God completely unsung. This book is dedicated to them.

Blessed are those who, going through the vale of misery use it for a well: and the pools are filled with water. (Psalm 84.6)

---

4 A quick trawl of the web following the BBC dramatization *Miss Austen Regrets* about Jane's rejection of a marriage proposal reveals almost universal surprise that Jane was not simply a cold fish uninterested in men or relationships. After all, it was her core material. Her biographer Claire Tomalin writes: 'As the years went by she knew that she didn't want to become a "poor animal", like her sisters-in-law and nieces, bearing yearly babies. Her books were her babies' (*Radio Times*, 26 April–2 May 2008, p. 14).

Chapter 1

'Ready for Sex'

Carla Weller is 16 and lost her virginity three months ago. A tall girl with a long, rather sad and watchful face – she has agreed to come to my house to talk. She arrives alone, brave, feigning indifference; obliging the mother of a friend who is helping me find informants. Carla is trying to find her way in a life circumscribed by state school and the public houses of Wood Green. Her mother is a barrister in Chancery Lane; her father, who is a Polish Catholic, is an artist. She loves her family very much, and would hate to upset them. She refers to her older sister's guidance, more than to her parents. Her answers to my questions reveal the habituated sophistication of a teenager suddenly, painfully, aware that her stock patter – the patter she used to use to shield her naivety – is false and inadequate. She is confused, hurt – and proud. She knows she's been made a fool of by a weak boy she did not love but with whom she had grown up. Curiosity got the better of her; she 'had sex' when she was told it was 'OK' to do so, i.e. when she 'felt ready' – yet now she feels, in some obscure way, she has demeaned herself.

As she talks, occasional gleams of girlish mischief twinkle in her eyes. They alternate with darker, petulant self-assertions that reflect an evident dawning awareness that sex is not just another childish prank. Sex leaves an emotional residue; there are social repercussions she had not anticipated, and for which no one seems to have prepared her. Pompous phrases straight from the teaching manuals thud into the space between us and lie like unexploded shells. The detonator is her dawning awareness that the system has let her down. Childhood friends who become 'sex partners' – or whatever the government calls them now – do not remain friends *or* partners for very long, it seems.

Carla: 'We have people come in and do talks about underage sex and that kind of thing. The whole awareness thing – they say, "If you are not ready for it don't do it"; wait until you feel comfortable. I won't put an age on it. You could feel ready and confident enough at a young age, but you should probably save it until you are slightly older because if you do get involved it could be a disappointment. It's hyped up so much by the media and by friends. It would feel a big deal – mainly to girls. Girls have a habit of talking more about their emotions. Boys are more, "Come on – get it over and done with" or "Oh, I would love to bang that!"

'I lost my virginity three months ago [*clicking her fingernail*]. In myself I was ready. I was ready for a while. It was more about making sure Jo was comfortable. I wouldn't do it unless it was a boyfriend. I would feel like a slut. There's not a real difference; it's more about myself. You need to feel a connection with someone. The one night stand appeals if you are drunk, in a club. To me it would have to have meaning to it rather than just wham bam thank you mam.

'I haven't seen Jo since it happened. It's probably a lot to do with his friends. Maybe he wasn't ready for the whole relationship thing. That's what's upset me. He is easily influenced, Jo is. He follows a lot of what his friends say, whereas I am the opposite. That was more curiosity for me. I was like, that's something I haven't done before. I just want to get it over with – see what it's like. We'd get onto the subject, me and my friends.. . . . At school they teach us that we have to feel ready. They tell us don't feel pressure. It isn't a need. If you want to do it, it's because you want to. Condoms. That was our biggest worry.

'To be honest? Because it was so hyped up, after the first time it didn't really. . . . it was really over-rated. I expected it to be amazing, oh wow . . . the media's always sex sex sex – something really massive in my life – but afterwards, I thought, well, that's done. My friends went the opposite way and went sex crazed, but it's not like I suddenly feel like I'm a woman now. The first time was during the day, the second time in the evening. I think Jo was curious as well. I didn't want to have sex with someone who had lost their virginity. I didn't want it to be a big deal to me but not to them.

'My feelings? I was nervous, there was excitement. Love? Well yeah, love has a lot to do with it but I wouldn't say at the time I was in love with Jo. I wouldn't say actual love, but I care for someone. I am more likely to call a girl a slag if she doesn't give a damn about his background. It must be a mutual decision to explore things you have never been involved in before. I don't think it has as much meaning when you are younger as when you are older. I don't know why that is. When you are young, you don't show the same affection: when you are a child you still have the whole do-you-fancy-him-thing. I think it's a type of love, but I don't think it's the same kind of love as when you are older. If you really are in love with someone, they will take you for what you are. It's not so much what you can give them – the whole virginity thing – it doesn't really matter to them. As long as you don't go around mentioning you have slept with someone already. What I have learnt from my sister, the guys don't like you bringing up past relationships.

'I would like to think of myself as not the kind of person who would have sex with any old Tom, Dick or Harry. With Jo, I really do care about him a lot – I won't say I am in love with him. He was more my friend, I had that sort of friendship, care for him. At school, they should go into the emotional thing. But it can scare you. It is going to affect you for the rest of your life. I think it would be good if they gave you emotional awareness rather than just "You can get an STD or get pregnant". I do think the emotions behind it are more important – because of how you feel after you have done it. I don't think I am a changed person. I am aware people might perceive me differently. "She's easy, she's the kind of girl that would have sex straight away". But I am really not.

'I don't regret that. If you are going to regret that, you are going to end up regretting it for the rest of your life. Having sex with Jo – it was OK. This is new for me and at first, I was a bit – do I regret this? and then I was – I would rather it was Jo who I have known rather than someone I met ten minutes ago.

'I can't tell you what love is because I don't know what love is. I am not sure what I have with Jo is.

[*Long pause*]

'At the moment I am really angry with Jo. I feel like he has pushed me out of his life and he hasn't given me a reason. That's what I wish they would have told me: "you will feel paranoid about whether the boy wants to be with you because he wants sex, or because he loves you." I wish they had warned us. My sister did try and tell me.

'You don't get taught about marriage as something for sex. They teach you that marriage is the final way to say I love you – not sex, which is interesting. Part of me wishes they had taught me that.

'He did tell quite a lot of his friends, which did upset me. They said, "Ah you've banged her now. Do it again. Do it again."'

Carla is a product of the national state school system. Her answers reveal a *faux* scientific attitude of moral neutrality in matters of sexuality. The education system and the research establishment operate a statistically based discourse that, while conveying authority, emerges from an ideologically closed circle of mutually reinforcing prejudice. Sex education is carried out within a framework of quantifiable data on health and hygiene. In itself, this can only incorporate 'risk behaviour' and 'undesired outcomes' rather than daring to break more metaphysical ground. Science, it seems, cannot guard the heart.

Society and its discontents

Seven million people in Britain now live alone, and lump it. According to the Office of National Statistics, this figure from a 2005 survey compares with three million in 1971.[1] More people than ever are living alone younger. The largest increase in single households over the past 20 years has been among those aged 25–44 years, more than doubling in the case of men, from 7 to 15 per cent. A further 58 per cent of 21–24-year-old males still live unwed, with their parents. The number of marriages has fallen from 408,000 in 1950 to 283,700 in 2005 – the lowest level this century. With marriage proving increasingly unpopular, it is assumed that most of these unwed people are permanently on the lookout for a sexual partner, or at least, for sex. If a woman goes to the doctor for her annual smear test, the first question she will be asked is not 'Are you married?' but 'What contraception are you using?'

For the post-Pill world, shame – the old way society maintained its boundaries – has been decoupled from sexuality. Shame has been deconstructed, and sex is no longer perceived to compromise social order but is as much subject to rational consciousness as any other appetite or human attribute. The Pill ended the infamous 'double standard' and freed women from unwanted childbirth, male domination and domestic incarceration to enjoy the pleasures of sex in the way men always had. Personal completeness

---

1   http://www.statistics.gov.uk/downloads/theme_social/Social_Trends37/Social_Trends_37.pdf.

now means sex. The famous City blogger Abby Lee exclaims: 'I feel like a woman again. Finally got some sex!'[2] For researchers and policy makers, sex is about safety and hygiene. Even the Girl Guides' new *Guide for Living for Modern Girls* has a chapter entitled: 'How to practise safe sex.'[3] For educators sex is a matter of biological maturity; just one way a person relates to another – and there is a menu of predilections. In 2005, 160,000 civil marriage ceremonies (marriages performed by a government official rather than by a clergyman) took place and accounted for more than two-thirds (65 per cent) of all marriages. Cohabitation before marriage is increasingly the norm. Whereas around 1 in 20 women marrying in the late 1960s had cohabited before their wedding day, by the end of the 1990s the figure was nearly eight in ten.[4] The liberation of female sexuality has helped the liberation of all forms of sexual expression including buggery, once regarded as demeaning and unmentionable.[5] Thirty years ago, there were just two venereal diseases – as they were known: gonorrhoea and syphilis. Today there are 23.

For the church, faithfulness and commitment still matter – but less so. Many in the church see their job as responding as sensitively as possible to people's 'needs', and affirming their chosen 'lifestyle'. Believers do not respond to God's calling; instead they choose their 'identity'. Clerical celibacy in the Catholic Church is increasingly discussed as 'optional'; the individual's choice rather than a calling.[6] Cohabitation is now regarded by influential

---

2   'Revealed! Britain's bestselling sex blogger', *Guardian, G2*, 11 August 2006, p. 9.
3   Radio 4 *Today* programme, 25 July 2007 interview with Denise King, Chief Executive of Girl Guides.
4   Duncan Dormor, *Just Cohabiting*, p. 3.
5   The National Survey of Sexual Attitudes and Lifestyles II, 2000–2001 (known as the Natsal Survey carried out by the National Centre for Social Research and sponsored by the Medical Research Council).
6   Several books have recently been published in the interests of 'optional celibacy': *Trespass into Temptation* by Gordon Thomas, published twice since 1986 is one; *The Unnatural Law of Celibacy* by R. N. Eberley in 2002 is another.

churchmen as an option that should have its own liturgies.[7] Pleasure in sex is, for the first time in 2,000 years of history, a serious theological and ethical issue, not a mere footnote in the age-long discourse on procreation. The Anglican Report *Marriage and the Church's Task,* published in 1978, speaks of 'a polyphony of love' that can be comprehended as, among other things, 'two individuals' experience of ecstatic pleasure'.

According to Duncan Dormor, Dean of St John's College, Cambridge, the Pill heralded the greatest social change since the ending of feudal society and the shift to a capitalist economy.[8] For Anthony Giddens, Tony Blair's adviser on marriage policy, this is a welcome sign of 'autonomous development', an aspect of 'a society where almost everyone has the chance to become sexually accomplished'.[9] Sexual morality has been replaced by sexual 'competence', defined by social scientists and statisticians as sex without regret or adverse consequences such as unwanted pregnancy or disease. The less regret there is, the more mature, socialized or 'autonomous' the individual is.

The implications of these changes in how society perceives its sexuality are significant, both for social well-being and for the increasing numbers of people for whom their status has no social meaning. They live in limbo, seeking artificial ways to palliate an inchoate sense of disconnection. Those who face life alone – the uncomfortably named 'singles' – have no status beyond a negative one: the not married, the uncommitted, the incomplete. They seek sex – and are assumed to be seeking sex – to make them complete. The historic option known as chastity is not just invalid as an ideal, but has effectively dropped out of the lexicon because few understand its wider social meaning. The supplementary role in

---

7 Dormor, *Just Cohabiting.*
8 Dormor, *Just Cohabiting,* p. 91.
9 Anthony Giddens, *The Transformation of Intimacy.*

parenting of the bachelor and the maiden aunt depended upon freedom and a notion of service. Now Aunt Jessie is likely to be too busy with her new toyboy. Respectability has withered on the vine since it is an attribute fostered by community activity. It has been replaced by individualistic 'acceptability' or 'cool'.[10] The anthropologist Tim Jenkins defines respectability as 'status claimed by an individual and his or her family, subject always to acceptance by the neighbourhood. It is a business of matching self-regard and public regard'. But the anonymity of the city renders pointless the social value of controlled or withdrawn sexuality.

It is the contention of this book that the absence of a rationale – and particularly a religious and social rationale – for the single state per se is an issue for us all. Miserable books – and there have been a plethora of late – that merely point out the isolation and despair felt by single people, compound the problem. Perhaps the most miserable of all has been Phillip Wilson's *Being Single* published in 2005, which contains analysis of 15 interviews with single Christian men and women chosen at random, all of whom found their condition wretched and pointless. Chapters like 'Loneliness, Dating and Sexuality' and 'The Challenge of Singleness'; and subheads such as 'The Biggest Problem of All', 'Church-Pain' and 'Church-Stress' speak for themselves. 'It seems that no matter the personality, the age, the context, or the church, loneliness is a simply enormous issue amongst many single people.'[11]

Wilson calls on the churches to 'do something' for their singles as if it were a a disease or a disability. In fact, it is more a sign of disordered times – and a pointer to the need for social reconstruction.

---

10   See Tim Jenkins' painstaking study "The Kingswood Whit Walk', Part III of *Religion in English Everyday Life: An Ethnographic Approach*, p. 78ff. Respectability, he says, is derived from the intimate interconnection between personality, territoriality and local history.

11   Philip Wilson, *Being Single*, 2005, p. 106.

At key times in the past it was the religious connection between chastity and the vitality of communities that gave purpose and meaning to the lives of the unwed. A restoration of such a connection is the key both to happier people and restored communities.

First, we turn to the contemporary social and emotional scene.

Parental accomplices

'We're from the ghetto!' smiles 18-year-old Nickie as I approach a group of teenage girls sitting smoking on the wall outside the St James Shopping Mall in downtown Edinburgh. 'We have a hard life,' she says smiling vacantly, between puffs on her smoke. I've explained – loosely – that I'm researching for a book on young women and their life choices. I offer to buy them a drink if they will talk to me. They march me to the nearest Burger King and I buy them Cokes. Beckie explains straightaway: 'My boyfriend bullies me, tells me what to do and that. I don't want to get married.'

I hope to talk to all four of them, but it's Nickie who sits down with me, while the others wait politely at another table, and giggle. They're not malicious; there is real prettiness in their faces and clothes, but they have an air of something slightly feral and disordered about them. It's what made me stop. Were they with the girl selling the *Big Issue* nearby, swaying slightly on her feet, losing her struggle to keep her eyes open enough to see the passing punters who might pay for the next fix? Perhaps they weren't with her – but they could have been.

I buy the Cokes – two politely refuse – and we stumble upstairs to find a quiet table. It is furnace-hot on this July heatwave day as I attempt to get my head around the presuppositions of a 16-year-old ghetto-child who's just been picked up by a middle-aged English woman and hasn't a clue what she wants. Pretty with a soft pink and white complexion, and the remains of a lurid pink hair dye an inch from the roots, she is guarded and almost totally lacking in self-awareness or sexuality. A child still – a naughty child – playing with dangerous toys.

Her dad died when she was 6, in a fire, she tells me. Her parents had already split up by then. He had come home one night dog tired, and had fallen asleep in the chair, dropping his fag on the floor. He died of smoke inhalation, trying to put it out. She had moved to Edinburgh three years ago with her mum, who found a job in a bakery. She attended St Augustine's Catholic school, although she was a Protestant. It didn't mean anything to her. She liked going on the Orange walks.

'I had a boyfriend for two years. It's someone to talk to, and spend time with and stuff. He moved to another school and it was too far to see him. I've never slept with a boy. The last boyfriend I had I was too young. Sex doesn't bother me. I'd sleep with him if I liked him. At school they just taught us about STDs and protection and peer pressure. If you don't want to do something don't get pushed into doing it, that's all they said. They didn't teach us it was wrong. It was in PSE – I can't remember what that means – it was guidance, all your work experience stuff, odd jobs, sex education.'

What are your hopes for the future?

'Getting money when I get older. Have a good job and be happy. I want to join the army. You have to be 17, so I will probably stay on at school another year.'

She looks at me as if I am strange:

'No – I don't think sex is for marriage. I don't want to get married anyway. I don't want to have any children either. I don't want to be tied down. I just want to have fun.'

What is fun for you?

'My pals, having a drink, going to parties – I drink vodka or anything – alcopops, WPB – I'll have four big bottles. If I really

want to get drunk, I will have a bottle of vodka to myself. I don't
do that every night.'

Why do you get drunk?

  'Because it's fun.'

Where do you get the money from?

  'From my mum.'

Schooled for sex

Between a quarter and a third of children now have sex at puberty,
and neither schools nor parents see it as their job to instil restraint.
The Natsal Survey, reported in the *Lancet* (see footnote 5), reveals
that 30 per cent of men and 26 per cent of women aged 16–19
years now reported their first heterosexual intercourse at younger
than 16 years. The proportion of women reporting first intercourse
before they were 16 had gone on increasing, it emerged, up to the
mid-1990s, but had 'stabilised' after that.

The report also noted a sustained increase in condom use and
a decline in the proportion of men and women reporting no contraceptive use at first intercourse with decreasing age at interview
i.e. younger and younger children are heeding the lessons they are
taught at school, and going into their first sexual encounters with
'protection'. 'Only a small minority of teenagers have unprotected
first intercourse.'

The report interprets the findings as showing that teachers
are the most significant influence on 'risk behaviour', noting
'an increase in the importance of school in the sexual education
of the young, particularly men'. It also notes 'a striking increase
in condom use at first intercourse', suggesting 'some impact' from
sexual health promotion messages, and concluding that '[f]actors
most strongly associated with risk behaviour and adverse outcomes
have considerable potential for preventive intervention.' Children
now know they can have sex without sanction – so long as it is

'protected' (and is therefore no financial burden on the State). Indeed, far from deterring them, they feel it's expected of them. A 13-year-old Tyneside lad stuck up his hand after a sex education class I attended, and asked: 'Miss – when you see condoms every-where in the toilets and shops and things, does that mean you've got to have sex?'[12]

Education, however, is not preparing children for the emotional rigours of the experience. Throughout the age range, there is a strikingly high level of regret – 42 per cent on average among females. Even among those whose first experience of first inter-course was 18 years and older, 19.3 per cent wished they had waited longer. 'Women' says the Natsal report, 'are twice as likely as men to regret their first experience of intercourse and three times as likely to report being the less willing partner.' Regret is one of four criteria of 'sexual competence' in the survey, but regret is an odd choice of word in the context of a subject that is treated scientifically, since it is usually applied to experiences that cause lasting harm. One does not regret one's first alcohol – one simply likes or dislikes it, unless one becomes an alcoholic. A schoolgirl may regret not revising harder for an exam – because the implica-tions endure into adult life. So too, first sex. The language belies the study's own purported neutrality.

The other criteria of 'sexual competence' are 'willingness, auton-omy and contraception at first intercourse'. A 'strikingly high proportion, 91 per cent of girls and 67 per cent of boys aged 13 to 14 years at first intercourse were not sexually competent'. However, '[a]nalysis by age group shows that sexual competence at first intercourse has increased during the past three decades, despite decreasing age at intercourse'. Kids have sex younger, use condoms more and claim less to be doing so under pressure.

---

12   State Secondary School, Long Benton, Newcastle, 16 October 2006.

There is an emotional and social cost to the relaxation of sexual mores in Britain that may be just as high as disease and pregnancy – but is harder to quantify. There is a clear correlation between sexual activity in young women, early school leaving age – and subsequent pregnancy. 'These data identify a vulnerable group of women in public-health terms; 29 per cent of sexually active young women in this study who left school at age 16 years with no qualifications had a child at age 17 years or younger.' For nearly a third of young sexually active women (29 per cent), future options are diminished.

This survey shows, beyond much doubt, that girls are having sex as young as possible, and that while more of it is 'protected', young women still pay the highest price. The ghost in the machine is clearly the school. The researchers applaud the increase of condom use – 'risk reduction' – and 'the association between school sex education and risk reduction' – irrespective of the emotional and social harm that's being done. Unhappy children mean an unhappy society. There is a significant group of young people whose aspirations are being betrayed by actual experience, whether thanks to parents, school, media or peers. Given the indisputable influence others have on the timing and mechanics of first sexual experience – as the report indicates – there is a clear role to be played by the whole of society in helping children to imagine an alternative route through the rapids of puberty.

Old singles: menopause, spinsterhood and the fear of dying

Fewer than 1 per cent of people marrying today are virgins.[13] The British Household Panel Survey carried out life-history

---

13   Dormor, *Just Cohabiting*, p. 2.

research into four groups of women born in the 1900s, 1920s, 1940s and 1960s. It found that while 17 per cent of women born in the 1920s had neither married nor cohabited by the age of 30, for those born in the 1960s the figure was a mere 8 per cent.[14] According to the 2000 Natsal Survey, however, for those born in the 1970s that figure had become negligible.

The Gadarene rush to have sex as soon as possible is powered partly by the myth of the miserable spinster. It is the myth that stigmatizes, goading younger women into false behaviour, forcing them to work harder at their own self-gratification than at creating supportive communities. This can only rebound on society, as more and more singles face a future stripped of nurturing forms of community. Says Christopher Hayes, Director of the National Centre for Women and Retirement Research in Southampton, New York: 'As the first baby boomers turn 55 . . . gerontologists expect the ranks of older singles to continue to grow, making this an issue for women in particular. My perception and it's a very strong one, is that singleness will be one of the biggest quality-of-life issues for women entering retirement in the millennium.' In the States, with 40 per cent of all adult women now single, says Kim Campbell, '[w]e are going to be living in a singles society.'[15]

Barbara Dafoe Whitehead, Co-Director of The National Marriage Project at Rutgers University, New Jersey says: 'There's no script for them to follow or borrow from an earlier generation of women . . . They're defining this stage of life as they go through it.' This new cultural phenomenon is invisible – most advertising is directed at couples. 'That means that 43 million women are invisible!'

There is a lack of a shared cultural image of the happy single. Kay Trimberger, a professor of women's and gender studies at

---

14 Central Statistical Office, *Social Focus on Women* (London: HMSO, 1995), p. 13.
15 'Beyond Bridget: A fuller view of single women' by Kim Campbell in *Christian Science Monitor*, 12 April 2001.

Soroma State University, California, says this may have to change. 'One thing that might help younger single women feel more secure in their singleness is more images of older single women. They need to focus not on a search for "Mr Maybe" but on "a single woman's pursuit of happiness".[16]

That pursuit is not new, of course, and, indeed there has been a small but influential secular literature since the 1930s, some of it recently republished, celebrating the turns it might take. The most influential writing is American, ranging from Marjorie Hillis's demurely hedonistic *Live Alone and Like It*, published in 1936 and republished by Virago in 2005, to Cosmo founder Helen Gurley Brown's famous *Sex and the Single Girl* published in 1963, foremost in the genre. Laurent Cantet's sensitive 1973 pre-AIDS film *Heading South*, about rich American women of a certain age finding illusory comfort in the boys who hang around a Haitian beach paradise, took Gurley Brown's ideas seriously and was re-released at the Edinburgh Festival in 2006. But the consequences he portrays are far darker than Gurley Brown intended.

Heading South

Ellen (Charlotte Rampling) is 55, an elegant divorced academic, who loves a beautiful young stud named Legbo for his ability to bring her to orgasm as soon as he touches her. Brenda – who never had an orgasm until she was 45, the summer three years ago when she came to Haiti with her husband and met Legbo – is depressed, on Valium, self-destructive and desperate. She's left her husband and her home, and come back to find Legbo; she admits to him one drunken night that she obsessed about him for three years 'in agony'. She explains to camera how he was just a boy they befriended on their holiday – when she finds herself unexpectedly

---

16   Ibid.

aroused by the beauty of his naked black skin as they lie sun-bathing together on a rock. 'I literally threw myself on him', she admits to camera.

Three years on, Legbo is making a career of his looks and Brenda returns to find him now the plaything of the mysterious Ellen – and of how many others? All the women seem to be vying for Legbo's favours, more or less overtly, oblivious to the fact that he has any other life. For these women, Haiti is a carefree paradise of sun and sea, of simple 'natives' and colourful markets. Haitians obligingly smile for their cameras, and the deferential poolside attendants flatter the women's egos, while massaging their sagging skin. Legbo's youth, smile, sweetness belie the dark world from which he comes, in which his mother lives in a shack, the police persecute poor street vendors just for kicks, and pimps and gang-sters roam the streets in shaded limousines. He is the women's plaything. Their money protects them from his reality, but it can-not protect him from them. The Haitian twilight world engulfs them all when Legbo's body is found dumped one morning in the hotel garden. He has been murdered by the henchman of his rich, jealous Haitian former girlfriend. Paradise is lost. Ellen returns to America; Brenda decides to continue her depredations on other islands – 'their names are all so beautiful', she says madly at the end as she sets sail for new conquests. Whatever your age, there is no consequence-free sex – though the consequences may remain out of sight and beyond the consciousness of those with money enough. 'Tourists never die', comments the police inspector bit-terly, as the body of Legbo is carted away. And yet these women, displaced, rootless, hopeless, are already soul-dead.

Exploitations compete in the film. Self-loathing and contempt form the film's sub-text. The barman Albert comments: 'Americans have worse weapons than cannons. Dollars. Everything they touch turns rotten.' American sex culture, driven now increasingly by women, is blind to itself, and destroys what it loves. The real mes-sage in *Heading South* is that sex, even post-menopause, is, for the unattached woman, a fool's paradise. Sex and death are linked. The arousal of old, fat or wrinkled white bodies by young, virile black ones, comes as a kind of a miracle of resurrection. But the miracle is illusory. Such sex, the film suggests, brings not life but death.

Yet, active sexuality among once 'respectable' middle-aged and elderly single women is increasingly flaunted. The largest relative increase in all the categories surveyed in the Natsal Survey was the number of heterosexual partnerships in a woman's lifetime, a figure that is still increasing. Nearly 20 per cent (19.4 per cent) of women in the 35–44 years age range reported having had more than ten partners, and nearly 10 per cent of 16–24-year-old women had had more than ten partners in the past five years alone. In 2000 nearly double the population than in 1990 now lived with a partner to whom they were not married – 17.3 per cent as against 9.6 per cent, despite the warning signs of instability in such relationships.

Where once it was considered surprising to discover older people had sex lives at all, now active extramarital sex among the over-50s is publicly celebrated. *The Daily Telegraph* announced with grim breeziness that 'reaching the age of 50 marks a fresh start for women who know what they want in the bedroom'.[17] 'Farewell frumpery, hello frolics', trilled Nicola Tyrer in a two-page *Weekend* feature about a new book – from America – called *Sex and the Seasoned Woman*. The paper accompanied the article with a coquettish picture of an elegant woman, naked but for pearls, lipstick and a scarlet hat, breasts demurely hidden behind the headline 'Sex at 50' and 2,000 words of prurient nonsense that would once have seemed more appropriate in *News of the World*. 'A great many women are finding "middlesex" more enjoyable than married life ever was in their thirties and forties, when juggling jobs, motherhood and what's-for-dinner guilt made for mostly exhausted sex.' There is The Widow who has since 'slept with six men, three of whom are up to 20 years her junior' and 'discarded' all but two, both of them considerably younger than her, and who met them all on the internet. And there is The Adulteress of whom Tyrer writes with relish that 'research shows that the best aphrodisiac for a menopausal woman is a new partner.' The article, which includes a side panel of pictures of 'models in their fifties', jokes that 'older handsets are more in demand than new ones'. The revival of model Twiggy's career in 2005 is cited as putting 'a spark back into Marks and Spencer and 50 back on the style radar.' Older women of the 1960s baby boomers generation have come back into focus because someone realized they are still 'hot' – mostly chemically induced by HRT. If you're not having sex with someone – anyone apparently – you're a frump. Sheehy's stories, says the standfirst, reveal that women who, a generation ago, would have been into knitting and doing good works are now into sex.

If this is equality, it is as usual equality on male terms. 'To make it in a man's world, you have to be one of the guys', concludes Ariel Levy in her brilliant *Female Chauvinist Pigs* published in 2005. Raunch culture, she writes, is about women out-manning the men. Where once only men could 'play the field' to the grave, now thanks to the Pill and HRT, women can too. Women don't want to be excluded from anything. And what's more, it's no good just bedding your pubescent hairdresser, young enough to be your son – you've got to make sure you get written about doing it. 'Appearing slutty and getting recognition for it are the fast track to heightened female stardom', writes Levy.[18]

British middle-class female exhibitionism still has a way to go – the British movie *Calendar Girls* showed no nipple, for all the scantily-cladness. But the elusive search for consequence-free sex fuelled by the media is likely to increase. One of the indicators is

---

18   Ariel Levy, *Female Chauvinist Pigs*, p. 144.

recent research into heterosexual anal intercourse. It has increased according to the 2000 Natsal Survey; 12.3 per cent of men reported having experienced it in the past year, as against 7 per cent in 1990 and 11.3 per cent of women as against 6.5 per cent. Anal sex is widely considered to be a good indicator of media influence on sexual behaviour, since it is not something people tend to speak about to each other.

Statistical evidence of reduced stigma and loss of shame attached to all forms of sexuality arising from economically driven patterns of social disengagement and media-induced conformism is borne out in conversation. In the following vignette, 'Celia', a 76-year-old bishop's daughter, describes the surprising turn her virginal life suddenly took, and her lack of regret for it, shored up no doubt by the view of her peer group in a once impeccably respectable church, some of whom told me that 'everybody does it' and 'chastity is such an old-fashioned idea'.[19]

Celia

Celia was already in her 40s when she met Lex and began an affair that was to span a quarter of a century – up to his death. A nursery school teacher who had failed to marry (as she puts it), Celia embodies the intimate connection between money and gender, the crude economic marginalization of women that impinged in a very practical way upon their emotional prospects. Celia's generation was the last to suffer this kind of victimization. Now 76, Celia came from a 'good' family – her father was the Principal of a leading Anglican theological college and later a bishop in the episcopal church in Scotland. Yet, she was nonetheless forced to

---

19 I spent two months in 2005 attending a particular Episcopal church in Scotland, during which the clergy kindly introduced me to as many 'singles' as I had time to interview. These are some of the ad hoc comments of older members of the congregation to whom I mentioned my project.

live in a twilight world of tied lodgings, digs and borrowed flats with almost no money, and even less social cachet. Unable through dyslexia to acquire more than a rudimentary education and then unable, as a single woman, to acquire a mortgage, she was forced to make a life on the scraps left over from the family table. With a small legacy once her parents died, she was eventually able to set herself up independently running a nursery – but by then it was too late to marry. In many ways she was lucky. Other respectable single women who lost their fiancés or husbands in the war and had no other family means to support them, were forced to enter service or seek menial jobs in old people's homes and mental hospitals with accommodation attached.

Celia got a post in the country at first, as nanny to a family friend, miles from the nearest town. She never met anyone vaguely interesting. Later, she lived rent-free in another well-to-do friend's unwanted flat in Edinburgh, looking after his child, but again, quite isolated. She was very poor. 'I used to take his gin bottles back to the shop and get tuppence. Three bottles of gin would buy you a loaf of bread.' Then she went to Beirut to child-mind for a British diplomat. She was expected to socialize with the other nannies, and again found it impossible to meet a potential spouse. Despite her background, she was never invited to the embassy parties. She remembers going to tea with one of the other nannies, and being shown the girl's latest purchase – a corset. 'I rebelled at that point. It was better just to be lonely.'

Her parents left her a little money when they died, and with it she set up a small nursery school, and for ten years she ran the school on her own. But by that time she was in her 40s, decidedly 'on the shelf' and wishing she weren't. Chastity was enforced – and resented. 'Everyone around one was quite happily having affairs, but not me.'

The conversation suddenly takes a startling turn I had not anticipated. I had imagined this strong-minded clergyman's daughter had been lined up to talk to me about the compensations of a virtuous life lived in the shadow of the bishop's palace, of the joys of self-sacrifice teaching children the faith. I had imagined she would tell me about at least finding within herself a 'stance' with which to counter the ravages of a secular sexualized environment. So I have to ask her to repeat herself: 'I had an affair for 25 years, and no one ever knew. But at least I waited.' This said with a penetrating look: 'I waited two and a half years.'

I try to absorb the fact that Celia is confessing, for only the third time in her life, to a passionate adultery with the husband of an invalid, that had lasted for a quarter of a century, and which she did not in the least regret. 'It was incredibly important. I was not sorry. I adored him. I would not have stopped for anything. Even when he dropped me for two years and came back again. I just was addicted to him completely, until the day he died.'

When pressed, she admits that perhaps it had compromised her 'slightly' – but she sees that compromise entirely in terms of her own fulfilment. 'I gave up a huge amount for it. I gave up having a husband, having children, having security. I don't know why everyone comes down on that sin, when you think of all the petty meannesses that people go in for. At least it's love and love is the most important thing.' However, she admits she felt 'unable to take communion' for three months after the affair began. But a family friend – Metropolitan Anthony Bloom – once told her on no account ever to stop taking communion. 'So I began again, and have never stopped since.'

I wonder how she would counsel younger people in the church; what line she might find herself able to take for the sake of future society more generally. 'I don't think I would give advice. I used to get really cross with that story of the early fathers, the one who was tempted all of one night and I thought, what does he know? Try being tempted for two and a half years!'

Of her faith, and why she is so very prominent a member of her respectable congregation, she admits: 'I believe less and less as I get older, but I get more driven that we have got to do things for people.' A kind of salvation by works, I suggest? She is not at all keen on Christ's saying of Mary that she had chosen the better part. 'Oh, I always felt so sorry for Martha. I never could stand Mary.'

Then I return to the question about advice to the young. 'I think it's so difficult now, I really, really do. How the young with all their hormones are supposed to cope, I don't know. But promiscuity is the thing I really, really hate. I think it does everyone harm. I don't know what I would say. Except please, please don't just drift into a sexual encounter, because it won't do you any good. In fact it will do you a great deal of mental and physical harm, but I can't say never before you are married. I think it should be thought about extremely carefully and not when you have had too much to drink!'

Celia in fact advocates exactly the same as the secular educationists who advised 16-year-old Carla.

I compliment her, before we leave, on her skin and hair. Despite her years, she is extremely pretty and still very feminine and very alive. 'Being cherished is good for the skin!' she smiles winsomely, as though Lex, who died nearly 20 years ago, is the love that still infuses her veins.

Celia who was pretty, well-born and unfairly spinstered, had done what she felt was her best. She tried mightily to resist the thing she felt she had been unfairly denied, and for which she longed with all her being. Her affair seems a world away from the grim reading of sexuality reports – and yet her discreet little hypocrisies and self-justifying evasions form the historic backdrop to our present discontents. Forced to battle against social prejudice and material deprivation, she survived emotionally in the only way that presented itself to her. The vaguely destructive ostracism faced by unmarried women of her generation found its compensation in a faithful unfaithfulness that is hard to condemn, even while it assaults the traditional morality of the church.

The stigma of virginity

Committed virginity is implausible in the twenty-first century, even while it makes increasingly good sense. The healthiest people in the country turn out to be never-married non-cohabiting single women – according to the government's *Focus on Families* report published in October 2007.[20] Nonetheless, Kate Wharton, an attractive 28-year-old, says the fact that she is a virgin is regarded as 'distinctly weird', and she finds it increasingly difficult to 'join in'. She attends a local evening class on sign language to be able to work with deaf people, and is astonished to find that girls her age and older – up to about 40 – 'don't have anything else to talk about than sex.' Even the way the sausage and mash is presented evokes sniggers. 'Our obsession with sex means we miss out on community, on genuine relationships, where "family" means more than just the people you are related to', she says. Even her mother opposes her: 'You will never get a husband if you are not prepared to sleep with a man', she tells her.

The pressure to conform to what is regarded as normal and healthy – despite the welter of statistics that prove sexual profligacy is anything but healthy – means that the non-conformists will face pressure and hostility. In a recent episode of *Casualty*, a Muslim doctor berates a nurse for advising an 18-year-old patient, a virgin who was nervous about having sex, to 'just do it, just bonk him'. But it is the Muslim doctor who comes across as offensive.

Germaine Greer observes, '[a]mong the consequences of the loosening of sexual mores is that the single state is now less respectable than it has ever been.'[21] And Claire Evans also comments: 'Sex

---

20   Office of National Statistics data derived from a number of sources including the 2001 Census. http://www.statistics.gov.uk/cci/nugget.asp?id=1870
21   Germaine Greer, *The Whole Woman*, p. 312.

becoming the norm has placed the social stigma that adultery and premarital sex once had onto celibacy. Virginity has become a spectacle.'[22] How has this happened?

---

22   Claire Evans, 'A Theological Response to the Issues of Singleness with 18–35 Year Olds in the Western Church Today', Undergraduate Thesis, London Bible College, 2001, cited in Kristin Aune, *Single Women*, p. 6.

Chapter 2

Made in the Image of Dog: Freud and His Disciples

Apparently I am 'single' because my jealous father so repressed my sexuality that I cannot relate to any man without associations of fear and extreme guilt. I choose not to indulge in one-night stands because I am trying to buy my way back into my father's esteem by being 'good'. My therapist is encouraging me to have sex with this guy to whom I am not married, with whom I am 'in love' but actually fear, and whom I have desired – and resisted – for six months, because it will free me from my father. Apparently, this being-in-love is a 'fantasy' and I should 'negotiate' with him the 'satisfaction of my needs' – instead of writing poetry about him. My therapist thinks we should have sex (with a condom) because it is healthy and a sign that I am sexually 'competent'. He comes from Angola and is 6'5". She says that what will hold us together is the acceptance by both of us 'until further notice' that we 'each gain enough benefit to make the relationship's continuance worthwhile'. Unfortunately, last night he forced himself on me without a condom, while I was 'negotiating' with him. Now I hate him, my father, and myself. And I may be pregnant and have AIDS. I clearly need more therapy.

(Anon)

The Western world is reeling from a series of social revolutions which have rendered absurd the practice of abstaining from or deferring gratification, particularly sexual. At best chastity is an eccentric 'lifestyle choice' for the jaded. At worst it implies, particularly for those who feel stuck with it against their will, a kind of social and emotional death. It carries the stigma of failure. If practised intentionally, in a way that links sex with the politics of morality, it implies an infringement of human rights. Occasionally a TV programme like *The Monastery*, broadcast in 2006, catches the public mood, and a sentimental regard for celibacy resurfaces, mostly as an atavistic romanticization of men in brown habits redolent of Cadfael. It is a mood that passes fairly swiftly however. The follow-up series *The Convent* was billed as 'therapy for the soul' – reverting swiftly to self-centred cultural type.

The sexual climate in which we now live, and whose implications have left family life in many urban areas at the point of 'meltdown',[1] has not happened by accident but is the result of ideological struggle. Foucault writes of 'the humanist dream of a complete and flourishing sexuality' – a sexuality no longer haunted by 'the sombre law that always says no'. The revolution in sexual ethics over the last century had more than one identifiable moment. For argument's sake, three such 'moments' of change are identified here: Freudian psychology; sociobiology, which identified sex with power; and the Pill, which radically undermined the relational context of sex and began the process of sexual engineering. As we study these 'moments' we come to see how politically contested sexuality has been; how little love has entered the equation – and how counter-cultural is chastity.

Freudian psychology

It is impossible to overestimate the ongoing significance of Sigmund Freud in contemporary European societies. Indeed, despite being

---

1 Mr Justice Coleridge in a speech to family lawyers at Resolution (formerly Solicitors' Family Law Association) in Brighton, 5 April 2008.

dead for nearly 70 years, Freud has recently been the subject of renewed interest, and new books are written on his work almost every year. Roger Scruton, in his updated survey *Sexual Desire* republished in 2002, writes that Freud's 'science of sex' (which he puts in inverted commas) has 'led to a greater revision in our moral attitudes than has accompanied *any* social upheaval or religious crusade'.[2] Freud still provides the general background to much of our received wisdom about sex and mental health, even though his work has been viewed with considerable scepticism, and is widely regarded not only as unscientific but even as mildly deranged. Scruton calls it 'myth' – a plausible way of explaining things – but since it is myth that describes itself as science, it therefore resists scrutiny by objective criteria. Words and ideas like 'sex drive'; 'libido', 'sublimation', 'neurosis', 'sexual repression', 'the ego', are all common parlance, part of the coinage of our understanding of ourselves – and all owe their origins to Freud. We accept them as fact, even though this is contested territory, incapable of proof. Our strong belief that sex is good for you per se; that our greatest joy comes from the 'convulsing of our physical constitution' (confusing orgasm with ecstasy); that the Victorians repressed their sexuality and were therefore hypocrites; that sex is a prime motivator and even the core of our personality, are Freudian reductions. That we are essentially animals, subject to unconscious, sexual and aggressive forces deep in the mind, that we can do little to control by our own volition, are Freud. That there are those who do control them but who are therefore distorted, evasive or mentally ill, is Freud. It is difficult if not impossible to defend ourselves against opinion that poses as fact. The foundation of the 'facts' of sex – or sexology as it is also called – are often little better than well-targeted guesswork, collapsed into and inspired by anti-religious spite – as we shall see.

---

2   Roger Scruton, *Sexual Desire*, p. 180 (my emphasis).

Says Scruton: 'Freud . . . was neither an accurate observer nor a plausible theorist'.[3]

It is important to grasp the hold Freud has on our contemporary mindset – and how difficult it is to recover alternative ways of seeing ourselves. Hard though it is to believe, given how Freud and Freudianism have so entered modern ways of thinking about sex, nevertheless, Scruton says, 'I believe [the inaccuracy and implausibility of Freud] to be both true and of overwhelming importance for anyone concerned to rescue sexual morality from the morass into which modern ways of thinking have enticed it.'[4] Scruton's unwieldy tome *Sexual Desire* is unfortunately almost impossible to understand, couched as it is in the abstruse language and academic references of professional philosophers but, given its importance to the discussion, it is crucial for us to try to translate what he's saying, after looking first at what Freud actually says.

Freud's work can be summed up in one sentence: 'Civilization, built on *religious* self-discipline, demands sacrifices in sexual behaviour that are harmful, especially to women.'[5] Though he does not prescribe alternatives, Freud's entire oeuvre – an altogether new discourse of apostasy and sexual freedom – lends urgent credibility and sanction to extramarital sex not just as *a* source of health and happiness, but the *only* source. Indeed, the very future according to Freud depends upon sexual licence, since civilization built on sexual renunciation is doomed to failure. 'Neurosis, whatever

---

3 Ibid., p. 196.
4 Ibid.
5 e.g. '[C]ivilization is built on the suppression of our drives' (*Civilized Sexual Morality and Modern Nervous Illness*, p. 90); 'If one looks at the real forms of nervous illness, the baleful influence of civilization is reduced essentially to the harmful suppression of sexual life in civilized peoples (or classes) by the "civilized" sexual morality prevailing in them' (Ibid., p. 88) etc.; 'we derive the opposition between civilization and sexuality' (*Civilization and its Discontents*, p. 45); 'Present-day civilization makes it clear that it will permit sexual relations only on the basis of a unique and indissoluble bond between a man and a woman . . . Only the weaklings have acquiesced in such a gross invasion of their sexual freedom' (Ibid., p. 40) etc.

its extent and whoever is affected by it, is liable to frustrate the aims of civilization and thereby actually to promote the work of the suppressed mental forces opposed to it.'[6] This is because monogamy produces weedy men who cannot legitimately vent their suppressed sexuality, and because female sexual abstinence before marriage results in neurosis after it. Freud writes: 'it produces well-behaved weaklings who later merge into the great mass of those who habitually, if reluctantly, follow the lead given by strong individuals.' Those who do not manage to channel their frustrated sexual drives into other – cultural – activities, either through poor constitution or lack of artistic and creative aptitude, 'succumb to neurosis'. Indeed 'they would have been better in health if they had found it possible to be morally worse', says Freud.[7] Religion has reinforced illness with its prescriptions and condemnations:

> Our civilization is built on the suppression of our drives . . . the single steps by which it has proceeded have been sanctioned by religion; any instinctual satisfaction that was renounced was offered to the deity, and the common property acquired in this way was declared to be 'holy'.

Only a minority do actually achieve that sexual abstinence which is required by civilization, however – and they lead the rest into misery. 'Most of the rest become neurotic or are damaged in some other way', Freud insists. And with a certain amount of contempt for the 'weak', he asserts: 'Experience shows that most of the people who make up our society are constitutionally not equal to abstinence.' Anyway, self-control in fact produces nothing much at all: 'I do not in general have the impression that sexual abstinence helps produce energetic, independent men of action or original

---

6   Freud, *Civilized Sexual Morality*, p. 103f.
7   Ibid., p. 94.

thinkers, bold liberators and reformers.' Having based his whole argument on the thesis that civilization with all its marvels and cultural accomplishments is the product of self-control and rechannelled sexual energy, he seems here to suggest that we would not lose much by rethinking what we mean by civilization after all. The learned doctor, poring over his scientific charts and diagrams, suddenly appears to be just an absent-minded quack who can undermine his own principal argument in a stunning *volte face* for the sake of a neat sentence.

Unfortunately, by this time, anyone struggling to be chaste while longing for an excuse to throw in the towel will see here their authorization. To have sex means I'm not weak, but sane, not neurotic, but independent and strong-minded – even pioneering enough to resist the social pressure to conform. Nothing much is risked by kicking over the traces completely. Any young *woman* reading this then finds her own nascent sense of rebellion confirmed as common sense. 'Especially obvious is the damage done to women's natures by the strict requirement of premarital abstinence', says Freud.[8] Women are especially at risk from 'civilization' and are merely shaking off the shackles of victimhood by having sex at will. Freud goes further: 'I think the undoubted intellectual inferiority of so many women can be traced back to the inhibition of thought that is essential for sexual suppression.'[9] Where before a woman was the 'angel of the house', the guardian of the sanctity of the hearth and the repository of family values and social stability, who must be protected in order to protect society, now she is merely weak. Her intellectual development is seriously constrained since sexual knowledge is the root of all knowledge.

Freud's final assault on chastity is to insult and humiliate the chaste: 'Many of those who boast of their success in remaining abstinent have been able to do so only by recourse to masturbation

8   Ibid., p. 99.
9   Ibid., p. 100.

and similar gratifications connected with the auto-erotic activities of early childhood' [he does not elaborate].[10] He now betrays his own repulsion and perhaps fear of sex, which assumes for him preponderance in the psyche beyond all reason, but he additionally infers a godlike knowledge of private human behaviour he cannot possibly have acquired, based merely on the information that some ('many') may have imparted in his consulting rooms. How many is 'many' when it purports to be 'scientific'? His own conservatism here is at odds with the fantastical flourishes of psychic conjecture and quasi-religious prophesy in which he otherwise indulges. While recognizing that religions, philosophical systems and ideals were the highest achievement of the human spirit, nonetheless, Freud says that we might 'deplore them as aberrations' since they are founded on delusion and lead to misery.

Freud can justifiably be regarded as the god of the 1960s; the deity, to use his own image, to whom abstinence is offered up. Abstinence becomes the guilt-offering of those who are made to see their strength as weakness, their virtue as vice, their self-mastery as gullibility. The emotional and physical continence by which they had built European civilization becomes criminal oppression. It becomes a crime against society to be good. Freud made people doubt their own minds, eschew their religion – and allow their children to vote for anarchy with their genitals. In describing, he prescribed. It became *political* to use sexuality as a weapon against patriarchalism and all its perceived evils. Civilization was no longer a place for the achieving of significant cultural objects but a prison to be smashed open. After Freud, Europe and particularly European Christian morality shrank back from itself.

Freud presented his views as though they were cold objective scientific findings, but made no overt prescriptions on the strength

---

10   Ibid., p. 100.

of them. He somewhat disingenuously disavowed the role of prophet at the end of his essay on mental illness, while nonetheless warning of an impending crisis in civilization if people did not have more sex! We live today with the results of his thinking. As Anthony Giddens observes, discourse shapes behaviour, even while purporting merely to describe it. By identifying human suffering with sexual repression, yet offering no other panacea than sex itself – by making so much of sex, in fact, Freud justified the sexualization of society, and, contrary to his avowed aims, the degradation of women. He underwrote a return to pagan wantonness.

Over the last century, in the pursuit of happiness, a trade-off has taken place between the cultural goods and safety of civilization and the pleasures of individual sexual licence. And we have called it science. We have deemed it obligatory to put up with a degree of sexual anarchy in the name of a spurious account of mental health, against the evidence of history, even though it endangers our very lives in community.

Modern people, particularly the young, are caught between the peer-driven, scientistically legitimated and educationally sanctioned imperatives of sexual activity – and the truth of their real feelings.[11] What they feel does not match what they're being told to feel – but instead of trusting their feelings, they disavow those feelings, believing them still to be attached to values they are taught to believe are outmoded, patriarchal and very dangerous. Those values are Christian.

Freud on faith

In his 1929 essay *Civilization and Its Discontents*, Freud launched a withering attack on religion. He is fascinated by what a friend

---

11 Scientism is science that has become ideological, a worldview, not the servant of a worldview.

has described to him as the 'oceanic' feeling of universal connectedness and well-being he has experienced.[12] The friend attributes
the feeling to 'religiosity and the impulse to religion'. Freud has not
experienced such a feeling and hazards a guess that, since religion
is nothing more than 'illusion', this feeling is a derivation of the
helplessness of the child and its longing for its father (a notion he
claims as 'irrefutable'). He is nonetheless interested in the nature
of this oceanic experience. He reckons it is bizarre to think that
we must rely on a sense of blissful connectedness with all of life
for our ideation of it, so the feeling must be something else. He
goes on to develop what become the building blocks of psychoanalysis – the belief (for that it surely is) that all of our past experience from birth onwards is 'still there' – that 'nothing is lost' – and
we can recover the various stages of our development that lie
hidden, like archaeological remains, in the 'id' or unconscious
mind. Psychoanalysis, the unscientific 'science' that Freud made
his own, based upon an *a priori* rejection of the transcendent
and our apprehension of it, thus becomes the reclamation of the
process of individual socialization undertaken from babyhood to
manhood. Part of that development is the separation of the ego
from the external world with which it is initially identified. 'The
ego is originally all-inclusive.' Thus, this oceanic feeling is a leftover
from infancy. He is convinced of this because in his studies of
the human psyche, he has come across examples of people some
of whom are more and some less 'separated' from the world around
them. 'Pathology acquaints us with a great many conditions in
which the boundary between the ego and the external world
becomes uncertain or the borderlines are actually wrongly drawn.'[13]
The formation of the 'self' can be affected, interrupted and so on.
Evolution in animals teaches that the self is more or less developed.

---

12   Freud did not qualify the word civilization, and his Eurocentrism further undermines his
      claim to be 'scientific'.
13   Freud, *Civilization*, p. 5.

Freud extrapolates from a theory he does not question in this essay, to the claim that human self development is a process of the more or less successful expulsion of negative sensations, and appropriation of positive ones: the absolute pleasure principle as he calls it. 'The fact that the ego employs exactly the same methods to expel certain unpleasurable sensations from within as it does to repel others from without becomes the starting point for significant pathological disorders'.[14] 'The retention of all previous stages . . . is possible . . . only in the mind'.[15] The mind in other words adopts its own programme for the attainment of happiness, a programme which is imposed on it by the 'pleasure principle'.

Civilization involves making the world useful and beautiful. Utility and pleasure – the twin goals – are the mainspring of all human activities. However, Freud cannot see how this applies to religion – how religion meets the utility/beauty criterion of civilization. So he hazards a somewhat bathetic guess: 'perhaps [it answers] to powerful human needs . . . that have developed only in a minority of people.' He then recapitulates the original point about the 'oceanic feeling' as the source of religiosity. He avers without compromise that the source of religiosity is in fact the child's feeling of helplessness, reinforced in adulthood, albeit pushed out of the foreground, by the fear of the superior power of fate. He concludes this essay with comments from an 'omniscient' friend (is he being ironic?) about the ability of the psyche in yoga to retrieve ancient or long-buried sensations through controlling the breath and stimulating certain organs. 'He sees in them a physiological justification, so to speak, for much of the wisdom of mysticism' – trance and ecstasy also. This is deeply materialist.

For Freud, religion is thus a form of mass delusion, a way of changing reality so we can live with it. But reality is social. In order

---

14   Ibid., p. 6.
15   Ibid., p. 7.

to change our own reality, the religious must change reality for others too:

> Religion interferes with this play of selection and adaptation by forcing on everyone indiscriminately its own path to the attainment of happiness and protection from suffering. Its technique consists in reducing the value of life and distorting the picture of the real world by means of delusion; and this presupposes the intimidation of the intelligence. At this price, by forcibly fixing human beings in a state of psychical infantilism and drawing them into a mass delusion, religion succeeds in saving many of them from individual neurosis.[16]

Religion is thus no more than one among several 'techniques' such as intoxication, withdrawal and so on, for making life bearable. Yet religion is uniquely culpable because – to Freud – it is coercive. Even though it has resulted in great achievements, it has done so at the expense of realism and happiness. Civilization is 'the sum total of those achievements and institutions that distinguish our life from that of our animal ancestors'.[17] Yet it is destroying us, and there is no solution. He abandons posterity to hopelessness and to the forces of a mythic unconscious we cannot rightly name or control, to our essential animal nature in fact. 'The child is father to the man' in the Freudian sense that we are not accountable for behaviours we adopted in our infancy, which still exert hidden influence on us. And more than that, those behaviours are themselves a hangover from our original caveman status. As mankind the animal evolved, so the child evolves. We must reclaim our essential animality because civilization has taken us too far from our true natures. Freud not only destroys the barrier between child and adult and thereby the barrier of responsibility for what we feel

16   Ibid., p. 22.
17   Ibid., p. 27.

and desire, he also reduces our spirituality to a derivative of mere sensation; locating it somewhere between the genitals and the will.

The system Freud developed is called psychoanalysis. It aims to help uncover our unconscious histories, premised not on any science of the mind, but on a self-referential system of observation and opinion reworked as metaphors of the mind's development. These metaphors take as axiomatic a framework of key ideas: that the mother is the first love object and that all sexual activity derives from the child's sexual contact with its mother; that religious disapproval of sex has to do with the father as competitor for mother love and so on. 'It's all about sex' as critics have put it.[18]

Freud's claims had no foundation in philosophy or ethics, without which they could not move beyond the level of mere personal opinion. Instead he had to try and ground them in an evolving theoretical framework, itself rooted in his work with those who came to consult him. In this way, psychoanalysis became a new closed discourse – a conversation with itself – bordering upon moral philosophy, but which eschewed much of traditional philosophy. Scruton describes this as 'the wildest fantasy'.[19] This fantasy has laid some of the foundations for influential critiques of modern patriarchy by feminists, and gays.

It would be wrong to give the impression that Freud's insights can simply be discounted. They cannot. There was real force in his concern for domestic unhappiness, its symptoms and undoubted roots in extreme sexual ignorance, guilt and shame. Female sanity was particularly at risk – and we shall examine this in another chapter. The hubris of the old European way of life that could result in two global wars within the space of 30 years was astonishing. A whole civilization clearly did need root-and-branch revision and renewal. Freud oddly was a self-appointed prophet, standing in for an unprophetic pre-Vatican II church which had acted as

---

18 See Leo Bersani's Introduction to the 2002 edition of *Civilization and Its Discontents.*
19 Scruton, *Sexual Desire,* p. 208.

mere chaplain to pain on the personal level and intellectual false-hood, stagnation and oppression at the public level. Freud's attack on the church reverberates to this day.

Some of the impossibility of chastity, post-Freud, derives then not just from Freud's assault on religion per se, but on a ferocious theorizing about the essential animality of the human person: 'sex the explanation for everything', as Foucault put it.[20] This denied any transcendent source to the human spirit, or the efficacy of grace in the formation of the personality as a response to it.

Towards the end of his life Freud moved beyond even the view that sex is redemptive of miseries caused by civilization, to a far darker belief that follows unremittingly the logic of his own thought. Nothing ultimately satisfies except the grossest kinds of bestiality; even non-monogamous heterosexual sex is a pale sub-stitute for pleasures *no* civilized society could permit – the sating of 'crude primary drives' which, prior to evolution, were anal and olfactory. Doglike, we gained maximum pleasure as quadrupeds by sniffing each others' genitals. Our sexuality 'fell' i.e. ceased to be convulsively satisfying, when we adopted an erect posture and saw each others' (ugly) genitals for the first time – which gave rise to shame. Shame led to disgust at previously satisfying genital odours associated particularly with faeces. Depreciation of the sense of smell became repression of 'the whole of his sexuality'.[21] Whereas the church had taught that mankind is made in the image of God, Freud taught that we are made in the image of dog. And if we seek joy, to dog we must return.

Foucault and the socio-biologists

Michel Foucault (1926–84) junked all this. But in debunking the Freudians, he set up an even more pervasive theory that has added

20   Michel Foucault, *The History of Sexuality Part 1. The Will to Knowledge*, p. 82.
21   Freud, *Civilization*, p. 43. Of the infamous note 1 from Section IV of *Civilization* Leo Bersani says, 'nothing is stranger'. His introduction to the Penguin edition published in 2002 – describes it as a 'descent into . . . fantasy'. I would add – madness.

fuel to the fire. Foucault created an opportunity he did not take; having debunked the repressive hypothesis, he said we were still captive to it. Writing in the 1960s, Foucault taught that a society so preoccupied with 'liberating' sex was in fact still in prurient thrall to it. Sex was still an issue of power, even if for the sake of pleasure and the money that could be made from it. The trick was to identify how sex is manipulable so as to free people to take control of it for themselves; to become sexually autonomous. Foucault aimed to complete what Freud started – to take the social out of sex altogether.

Freud identified sex as the core of the personality. Foucault took issue with that. Freud, said Foucault, gave the modern preoccupation with sex its most cogent formulation. Suddenly we defined ourselves by our sex – whereas apparently we had not been so preoccupied in centuries past. In the space of a few centuries, we came to 'direct the question of who we are to sex.' This meant 'sex as history, signification, discourse', said Foucault. 'We have placed ourselves under the sign of sex . . . [s]ex the explanation for everything.' But, far from being repressed, hushed up and hidden, sex had now become an all-consuming concern. Where the church had developed systems of examination and mortification in the confessional, 'scientists' had subsequently taken this up through psychoanalysis. This explained the subject's solemnity, he says! 'We are conscious of defying established power, our tone of voice shows that we know we are being subversive.'[22] 'Some of the ancient functions of prophecy are reactivated therein. Tomorrow sex will be good again.' What Foucault calls 'a discourse' evolved – a way of talking and of seeing. He likens this discourse to preaching – and calls it 'a great sexual sermon', part of a global evolution of happiness. If, says Foucault, the relationship between sex and power was characterized by repression, why was there so much written about it? He began to suspect that the present preoccupation with sex had piggy-backed on the Victorian obsession with

---

22 Foucault, *The History of Sexuality*, p. 6.

recording and categorization that it had inherited from seventeenth-century Enlightenment thinkers, for whom curiosity about everything was paramount. So it is simply a myth to call society sexually repressed when it had been 'loudly castigating itself for its hypocrisy for more than a century, speaking verbosely of its own silence, taking great pains to relate in detail the things it does not say, denouncing the powers it exercises, and promising to liberate itself from the very laws that had made it function'.[23] The critical discourse about repression, far from representing a historical rupture, was in fact just part of a process. The minute study of sexuality, crystallized and given its own authoritative literature by Freud, far from 'liberating' sex, actually generated increased forms of power through it. It was just a 'more devious and discreet form of power'.[24] Foucault's thesis is spelled out as follows:

> since the end of the sixteenth century, the 'putting into discourse of sex,' a mechanism of increasing incitement; that the techniques of power exercised over sex have not obeyed a principle of rigorous selection, but rather one of dissemination and implantation of polymorphous sexualities; and that the will to knowledge has not come to a halt in the face of a taboo that must not be lifted, but has persisted in constituting – despite many mistakes, of course – a science of sexuality.[25]

The current noisy proliferation of all kinds of sexuality, especially perversion, is a direct result of the 'putting into discourse' of sex in the Victorian era; that, far from being repressed, it became a matter for the minutest discussion and analysis, from which the present interest stems and on which it feeds. Sex was not driven underground in modern civilization, but preoccupied it, says Foucault. Far from being a 'liberation', the current preoccupations

---

23   Ibid., p. 8.
24   Ibid., p. 11.
25   Ibid., p. 13.

represent a vast imposition of power in all its forms upon the bodies of the public. Power is *focused* upon pleasure, rather than its opposite. Indifference to sexual exploits and their outcomes in the bodies of our children become the sign of a mature society at ease with its own sexuality.

Since the demise of the church, implies Foucault, many other groups or sectors in society have attempted to use their influence over our bodies in various ways and for various reasons. We have allowed the pursuit of pleasure, de-legitimated by the church, then 'liberated' by the Freudians, to be harnessed to other forces such as commerce, or any other factional agenda, leaving us no more free than when the church dragooned all sexual activity into marriage. And indeed, administrative power interferes with our sexual bodies from cradle to grave; through incitement of school-children to sexual activity 'when you feel ready'; to the ideological blurring of gender and sexual orientation by different sexual lobbies through the sanctioning by government of civil partnership; to the provision of inoculation for 9-year-old girls against cervical cancer. Foucault dreamed of a society in which interventions of *all* kinds ceased. Whereas Freud had made of the self a sexual body in relation to other bodies and to civilization, Foucault following Nietszche (1844–1900), whom he admired, wanted to return the sexual body entirely to the self in a utopian nightmare that could – and did for him – lead only to death.

One creates one's own sexual self, Foucault said. After Nietzsche announced the death of God, individuals were no longer under obligation to conform to a pattern set in heaven. They were free to fashion themselves in whatever way they chose. One's nature and one's values are not given; they are constructed. 'Let us,' Nietzsche urged his readers, 'be involved in the creation of our own new tables of values ... we want to be those who give themselves their own law, those who create themselves!' 'One thing is needed,' he declared, 'to give style to one's character – a great and rare art.' And the way to do this, he insisted, was by unlocking the

'Dionysian' element in one's personality – the wild, untamed, animal energy within, one's own personal *daimon*. 'Man needs what is most evil in him for what is best in him.' Only by exercising 'the will to power' could one discover true transcendence.

James Miller has described Foucault's life as 'a great Nietzschean quest' to explore the extremities of experience.[26] Foucault believed that only through excess could creativity and the intensity of joy be known. As a young man his experience of homosexuality, madness and suicide and incarceration for a time in a mental institution prompted a lifelong attempt to validate and reincorporate all such experiences. He believed that no one had the right to reject or marginalize another and that attempts to do so were simply forms of power to be resisted. In *Madness and Civilisation*, for example, he explores the dark, excluded side of human nature, of sadomasochism, war and irrationality. He became the champion of all that had been disallowed by society. His whole persona, mad, gay, morbid became his intellectual project. His own self became overtly the arbiter of what was worth studying and prescribing.

> Whenever I have tried to carry out a piece of theoretical work it has been on the basis of my own experience, always in relation to processes I saw taking place around me. It is because I thought I could recognize in the things I was, in the institutions with which I dealt, in my relations with others, cracks, silent shocks, malfunctionings . . . that I undertook a particular piece of work, a few fragments of autobiography.[27]

Foucault's thought resonates profoundly in all those, especially the young and the outcast, who long to be free of the shackles of moral constraint.

---

26   Citations from James Miller, *The Passion of Michel Foucault*, 1993, in John Coffey, 1996, 'Life after the Death of God: Michel Foucault and Postmodern Atheism', *Cambridge Papers*.
27   Michel Foucault, 1988, *Politics, Philosophy, Culture: Interviews and other Writings, 1977–1984*, (New York; London: Routledge), p. 156.

He sought out the far reaches of experience – 'expérience limite'. He became fascinated by de Sade, by sexual cruelty and the link between the erotic and death. In the 1970s he moved to California to take up a position at the University of Berkeley where he had his first experience of LSD and immersed himself in consensual sadomasochistic sex (S/M). The gay bars and bathhouses of San Francisco gave him the opportunity to put into practice the theories of de Sade. He openly espoused the 'virtues of sado-masochism' as 'a creative enterprise' in which participants invented new selves by exploring new possibilities of pleasure'. But this was the time of the advent of AIDS. 'To die for the love of boys. What could be more beautiful?' Foucault had once asked. 'One should work on one's suicide throughout one's life', he stated on another occasion. John Coffey suggests that Foucault pursued his own death by disease. 'By throwing himself with reckless abandon into the bathhouse scene when the spectre of AIDS was becoming clear . . . Foucault may have been trying to achieve a fitting climax to his life, one which fused his great obsessions: madness, perversion, torture and death.'[28]

Foucault articulated with all the elegance of a literary genius the pent-up post-Christian rage of those whose activities and lusts the church had ever disallowed or condemned. He summoned from the shadow side of a centuries-old civilization all the demons of sex and death – and bade them sing. His work is still the acme of academic fashionableness. He has been required reading for a generation, despite what he excluded – which was love.

Giddens and 'plastic sexuality'

Freud taught us to be self-conscious – conscious of ourselves as *selves*, as personal histories that we can control, interrupt, manipulate, change. It is fair to say that before Freud the self did not exist

---

28 John Coffey, 'Life after the Death of God? Michel Foucault and Postmodern Atheism', December 1996, *Cambridge Papers* published by the Jubilee Centre.

in the terms in which we conceive it today. Not only that, but he taught us to understand this self in terms of a difficult-to-negotiate *sexual* history. In psychoanalysis, one is taught to see one's personal history as a *sexual* history, fraught with forces that control us ineluctably. There is no alternative narrative.

Psychoanalysis gave us a language and tools to dig into our personal histories, and find there the problematized *sexual* roots of our identity. Because Freud's work emerged from the clinician's couch, all sex and indeed all personality has been tinged ever since with the language of malady. If to be healthy and happy *is* to realize oneself sexually, according to Freud, then sexual abstinence must be essentially pathological. Freud made us suspicious of all our relating and loving – but more especially of our self-control. Abstinence is especially vulnerable to a 'hermeneutic of suspicion'.

Foucault changed the emphasis from pathology to pleasure – then linked it to power. In this framework, sexual perversion declines, first to become deviance, then to become simply pluralism.[29] From there it is only a short jump to the conclusion that the only true perversion now is abstinence. Much extreme sexuality in contemporary literature is an attempt to take literally the Sadian/Foucauldian manifesto that what is truly shocking is our own complicity in power. We can gauge the extent to which we are truly free by our indifference to obscenity – or rather, to what others deem to be obscene.

Anthony Giddens, sociologist and Director of the London School of Economics, recasts Freud and Foucault in the arena of 'love' – but it is a word he uses in inverted commas. Giddens, as keen as his mentors to be memorialized in the striking turn of phrase, especially if it can be made to mean the opposite of its original Christian derivation, gives us 'plastic sexuality'; 'confluent love' and most remarkably, 'the pure relationship'. These are all ideas that owe their origins to Freudian self-consciousness and

---

29   Havelock Ellis took up an exploration of this.

Foucauldian postmodernism, and which totalize the humanist dream of personal autonomy and consequence-free sex. 'Confluent love' exists where adults of any gender or orientation negotiate their relationships on the basis of equal power and equally negotiable satisfactions. There is no need for marriage or taboo because all people are now equally free to express their desires, whatever they are, and have those desires met. 'Confluent love develops as an ideal in a society where almost everyone has the chance to become sexually accomplished', says Giddens, who evidently lives on some other planet where live no mortals with halitosis, dandruff, clammy hands. The 'pure relationship' has nothing whatsoever to do with virginal damsels or virtuous endeavour; quite the reverse. The pure relationship is one which is entered into for its own sake, for what can be derived by each person from it – not until death do us part, but 'until further notice'.[30] It is continued only in so far as it is thought by both parties to deliver enough satisfactions for each individual to stay within it. The 'pure relationship' has replaced marriage as the arena in which love is tied to sexuality. It is, in other words, the opposite of the Christian understanding of purity. It presumes the disappearance of the schism between 'respectable' women and those who in some way lie outside the pale of orthodox social life. It is sexual love shorn of shame or caveat. Guilt and singleness are both unnecessary categories, for such usage is a manifestation of a lack of 'competence'. 'Now that conception can be artificially produced, rather than only artificially inhibited, sexuality is at last fully autonomous.'[31] Obsessions, predatoriness, womanizing, etc. are all instances of 'an incoherent narrative of self' – created by a patriarchal society which can be rectified. In a postmodern society, where the male no longer needs to dominate, the need for 'sexual conquest' ceases to be meaningful. 'Confluent love presumes intimacy: if such love is not achieved,

---

30   Anthony Giddens, *The Transformation of Intimacy*, p. 63.
31   Ibid., p. 27.

the individual stands prepared to leave'[32] – presumably without regret or grief in Giddens' calculable, bloodless society.

There is much in Giddens' solemn and influential analysis that is beyond parody, born as it is of the po-faced suburban intellectualism of the contemporary left. The deracinated boy from the faceless suburbs of north London exhibits a facile if seductive dexterity with ideas that catapulted him to the highest echelons of academic and political influence. And yet his writing lacks both depth and background. It is the glib word-smithing of a clever university-educated drone who believes in nothing, and has little to fight for. It is rootless, gutless, passionless – and appeals to the millions of impressionable, footloose teenagers from all over the world who pass through the glitzy gates of the London School of Economics. *The Transformation of Intimacy* is a set text. It appears edgy and brilliant. But just as the famous Kinsey Reports 'became constitutive of the social reality they portray' so with this.[33] When Giddens says: 'The self today is for everyone a reflexive project – a more or less continuous interrogation of past, present and future' his description becomes plausible authority enough. In the urban jungle, the 'Who am I?' question, intimately tied up with the question of relationship and lifestyle, actually begets no answer because no one hangs around long enough to answer. I need a story to tell about myself . . . but since my self is my sex, my story must concern only my sexual relationships. But true relationship needs continuity. In *The R Factor,* Michael Schluter analysed continuity as one of the five key building blocks of a healthy relationship. Yet in Giddens' urban dream, continuity is implausible because it is costly and therefore inconvenient. This *self/sex* about which I tell a story is now infinitely variable, or malleable since contraception has given me total control of it. I can change at will; I do

---

32   Ibid., p. 84.
33   Ibid., p. 28.

not need to encounter resistance or pain if I do not wish to. I can quit, or move.

'Plastic sexuality', says Giddens, has been pioneered by gays and women. Sex is no longer linked to procreation. Conception now can be not only *controlled*, but artificially *produced* in the lab. This is the final liberation for sexuality which thence can become wholly a quality of individuals and their transactions with one another. Gays have pioneered the 'pure relationship' – a relationship without the traditionally established (i.e. patriarchal) framework of marriage and in conditions of relative equality between partners. He refers to a study in the late 1970s cited in the Kinsey Report that showed that of 600 male homosexuals in the US, 40 per cent said they had had 500 or more sexual partners.

> The term 'gay' . . . brought with it an increasingly widespread reference to sexuality as a quality or property of the self. A person 'has' a sexuality, gay or otherwise, which can be reflexively grasped, interrogated and developed.

The gay lobby has led the way in the debate about 'sexual lifestyle' – where identity is a property that can be chosen and where we need give no account to society for such choices or the actions they lead to. But this is a hellish vision that not only leaves the singleton out altogether, but which leads only to further social fragmentation, isolation, barbarity and madness. As Scruton says: 'The maximal self does not exist in the state of nature, but only in society, and is sustained by custom, habits and beliefs that are easily destroyed, and which we destroy at our peril.' I have an effect on those around me; I owe something to the society that nurtured me, and to which I owe my health and happiness. It may be better if I behave or abstain from behaving in certain ways. I am a 'person' – that is, an 'entity with agency and answerability', not simply a body with needs. Any other vision brutalizes both me and those around me – and ultimately diminishes all our chances of growth and fulfilment.

Hence the present misery of the singleton. In what sense of the various senses we have analysed can a single person be said to 'have a sexuality'? In what sense is chastity a 'lifestyle choice'? Chastity is paradoxically a sin against the society of autonomous individuals. It is a failure to choose – but the choice as it is presented to us is not a real one. By living – and loving – without sex we give the lie to the bogus Giddens discourse. Giddens' vision destroys particularity; insists on dispensability. Singletons have been written out of the discourse. We do not exist – and do not deserve to exist. If discourse shapes reality, the chaste have been 'talked' to death.

Chapter 3

Sex and the Destruction of Childhood

Family breakdown is on a scale, depth and breadth which few of us could have imagined even a decade ago. It is a never-ending carnival of human misery. A ceaseless river of human distress. I am not saying every broken family produces dysfunctional children but I am saying that almost every dysfunctional child is the product of a broken family.

Mr Justice Coleridge[1]

We are more confused than de Sade about the relationship between power and pleasure . . . at least he has the merit of resolving the contradiction between the maximizing of pleasure on the one hand and exploitation and abuse on the other. Because of our failure to recognize this contradiction, we live in a world where criminal expressions of sexual pleasure – in rape, for example, and child abuse – are continually being agonized over, apparently with little understanding and to little effect. (Jenkins: 'On Lust')[2]

---

1 Sir Paul Coleridge, High Court Family Judge, in a speech to family lawyers at Resolution (formerly Solicitors' Family Law Association) in Brighton, 5 April 2008.
2 From a 'Sermon on Lust' given by Rev. Tim Jenkins, Dean of Jesus College, Cambridge at St Mary's, High Pavement, Nottingham, 22 March 1992. Unpublished.

Desire today knows no social bounds except physical health – and for some the dangers of disease and death merely add to the experience. There are few rules, except those we succeed in establishing for ourselves – which for the weak, the disturbed and especially children is increasingly difficult and damaging. The infamous 'double standard' has not been abolished; it's simply been socialized. The dark side of sex was once kept private. Married men could indulge themselves in sexual proclivities or with a mistress so long as they were discreet about it, while women kept the home unsullied from base desire. Public morality was a code that people observed, and suffered the penalties. Now the social and political ambition is for all to behave like men have done in sexual matters, i.e. without conscience. The harder we try to realize this fantasy, the more the shadow side of sex falls on women and more especially children.

This chapter begins with a quote about the Marquis de Sade (1740–1814), who saw perhaps too graphically what Europe was doing in ridding itself of religion and a religious-based ethic. The killing of the French King Louis XVI in 1792 marked the ending of an experiment in Christian society, in which, at least hypothetically, every person mattered equally in the sight of God. The King represented the presence of the soul in the body politic, guarantor of the ideal of divine justice. With the king dead, the social conscience was dead and what remained was freedom and 'free thought' – schemes that made man the measure of all social and moral order. The Marquis de Sade, writing up his extreme sexual experiments at this time, gave expression in bitter parody, to the new truth. He said, first, that a society born out of the destruction of a God-ordered hierarchy must be based upon and permeated by crime. Crime is its truth, since there is now no collectively guaranteed compunction against it. And second, that what comes to replace the former hierarchy is a society of Masters and Slaves, a return to the unmediated power of Ancient Society, where some are persons and others are not, but simply objects at the disposal of these persons. And he joins together these views in a savage parody of Natural Man.

> All our desires and pleasures should be fulfilled, and since perversity heightens pleasure, and can only be natural, for it arises within us, it too should be given full reign. Moreover, society should be ordered politically in order that these pleasures should be pursued to the utmost. And this can be carried out because it is a natural truth that the strong dominate the weak, and the truth of such a society is criminality.[3]

The consequences of this are upon us, not just in lives blighted in the obvious ways, but in the hidden legions of compulsion victims who are increasingly defenceless against their demons in light of the insidious temptations of cyber-sex that can lead to despair and suicide. Late-night work alone on the computer; round-the-clock mobile phone prompts about improving your sexual thrills, which evade the spam filter, the breathless anonymity of the city, all mock the rickety barricades of the irresolute mind. In a leader column entitled 'Porn's Stranglehold' for the US's *Christianity Today* magazine, Editor Timothy Morgan writes that 70 per cent of American men aged 18–34 admit to viewing Internet pornography once a month. Eight per cent of adult men and 3 per cent of women in America have become sexually addicted – roughly 30 million Americans hooked on the neurochemical response of the body during sexual behaviour, often acquired in teenage years. New faith-based addiction recovery groups are springing up all over America – 60 at a recent count.[4]

Comedian Russell Brand tells us he was initiated into sexaholism by his father in the brothels and by the sex slaves of the Far East when he was 17. What began as a jaunt, a sleazy, latter-day

---

3 Jenkins, 'On Lust'
4 'Help for the sexually desperate' in *Christianity Today*, March 2008, pp. 28–35

rite of passage into adulthood became a compulsion he could not stop on his own. 'I'd been confronted with the galling reality that there are things over which I have no control and people who can force their will upon you,' says Brand in his recent autobiography. Brand had been taken to Hong Kong by his dad.

> His third marriage had just broken up, so he needed someone to go on holiday with. I was unemployed, penniless, birdless and desperate for his approval; we were the perfect holiday companions. In addition to Hong Kong we visited Bali, Singapore, and Thailand, and in all those places we saw incredible things . . . On day one, we went to some sleazy dive hidden behind a thick black drape where women from the east traipsed louchely along the mirrored promenade in garish beachwear. That promenade was a conveyor belt from which produce could be selected; . . . My dad sat there next to me, familiar with this glistening and foreign terrain . . . I didn't understand what I was witnessing, but by jingo, I knew I liked it. Dumbstruck, I sat looking at the women . . . they didn't seem enslaved or exploited – to me they weren't; they were mistresses, goddesses, salvation. I can't wait to tell my mates . . . I said to myself.[5]

Brand and Brand-père had money, power and status. Their sense of power was enhanced by sex. As he admits: 'Sex is recreational for me, as well as a way of accruing status and validation'. Brand does not blame his father for his addiction. He does not seem particularly interested in reflecting on it at all. It's just a part of the narrative of celebrity life.

Many parents do not know what to condone and what to condemn. Sometimes they are expected to condone and condemn

---

5   Russell Brand, *My Booky Wook* (Hodder & Stoughton, 2007).

the same thing at once. The Edinburgh daily *Metro* is the free paper distributed on Edinburgh's buses. It is not targeted at the middle and upper classes, who do not travel by bus, but at the poor and schoolchildren, who do. On 21 August 2006, page two carried a news-in-brief: 'Sex book set to rock Parliament'. It told of a senior Tory who 'romped with prostitutes and watched as a lady-boy pleasured his friend'. The story describes this as 'a shocking new political memoir'. The book, *Unzipped*, is, according to the salivating *Metro*, 'so graphic it has "adults only" printed on the cover'.

Yet on the next page of the newspaper is a full-page article surrounded by five colour pictures of grinning nude and semi-nude men with towels draped as suggestively over their genitals as possible, and a large close-up of a woman's ample cleavage – with the headline 'Bluff or buff'. It tells the story of an April Fool organized by the betting company Paddy Power, who 'thought it would be funny to announce plans for a world strip poker tournament – without there actually being one'. So many readers took it seriously that the company decided to run the tournament anyway – at the Café Royale in London. 'It was a real party atmosphere' quotes the story. 'It was supposed to be a walk of shame for all those eliminated. But most people seemed to enjoy the streak – the chaps, especially, were having a joyful time on the top of tables, swinging their towels around their heads'. For 'removing his last piece of clothing' the winner, a 32-year-old writer from Slough, won £10,000 – and a further £10,000 went to charity. A total of 195 players took part in this spectacle – 127 men and 68 women – from 12 countries.

'Emancipation', writes Anthony Giddens, 'is separate from permissiveness in so far as it creates an ethics of personal life which makes possible a conjunction of happiness, love and respect for others'. Respect here is slippery, implying as it does, individual 'autonomy' without social restraint – indifference in other words. All the participants at the Café Royal were evidently happy, and mutually respectful, since they had chosen to be there. So what makes 'fun' stop being 'joyful' and become 'shocking' instead? Why should we be 'shocked' at the 'pleasuring' by a consensual rent boy of a gay politician, yet find funny the naked romps of adult men for money in a public restaurant? When it involves children? Yet, in 1948, Wilhelm Reich, the influential psychoanalytical radical gave particular attention to the 'sexual rights' of children and adolescents. He wrote, in *Listen, Little Man!* – in capital letters: 'YES, WE WANT OUR SONS AND DAUGHTERS TO BE OPENLY HAPPY IN THEIR LOVE INSTEAD OF ENGAGING IN IT CLANDESTINELY, IN DARK ALLEYS AND ON DARK BACKSTAIRS'.[6] Giddens interprets Reich thus: 'Children are to be given the right to engage in sexual play with others and to masturbate; they are also to be protected from the domination of their parents. Adolescents are to have the opportunity to fulfil their sexual needs in an unbridled way, in order that they might be the agents of future social change'.[7] A 'ladyboy' who pleasures senior Tories is no longer a crime committed by adults on the vulnerable, but a child fulfilling his own sexuality. Why therefore be 'shocked'? Why not be joyful?

Indeed Reich's view does not shock Giddens, the government's family adviser who, while acknowledging that Reich was controversial, says 'Sexuality is undoubtedly the key to modern civilization . . . Sexual emancipation . . . is effectively understood as the radical democratization of the personal. Who says sexual emancipation . . . says sexual democracy'.[8] For Reich, says

---

6 Wilhelm Reich, *Listen, Little Man!* (first published in 1948), this edition 1975, p. 95.

7 This is Giddens' interpretation of Reich in *The Transformation of Intimacy*, p. 163. It compounds what, in the original, was a kind of post-holocaust hippy-sensibility that dreamed of utopia but which, in Giddens, becomes a manifesto. In Reich, it led to imprisonment (he died in the federal penitentiary in 1957). In Giddens, such thinking led to the House of Lords. In the original, Reich writes of a future when 'your adolescent daughter's happiness in love will delight instead of enraging you; when you will only shake your head at the times when one punished little children for touching their love organs; when human faces on the street will express freedom, animation and joy and no longer sadness and misery; when people no longer will walk on this earth with retracted and rigid pelvises and deadened sexual organs' (p. 105).

8 Anthony Giddens, *The Transformation of Intimacy*, p. 182.

Giddens, 'modern society is patriarchal and its emphasis upon monogamous marriage serves to develop authoritarian traits of character, thereby supporting an exploitative social system'.[9] In order to achieve a society in which all, children included, negotiate their sexuality freely on an equal footing 'society would have to undergo a thorough-going upheaval, and a great deal of psychic change would also be necessary', says Giddens. Fortunately for us '[w]e have no need to wait around for a sociopolitical revolution to further programmes of emancipation . . . Revolutionary processes are already well under way in the infrastructure of personal life'.

And he is right. The media are a tremendous ally in the serious business of emancipating our children from any authoritarian constraints that might in fact protect them from predatory politicians and perverse sociologists. MTV, the station of choice for today's teens – it's the default channel in many of the nation's gyms, bars and cafés – ran a documentary called *Virgin Diaries* in which ten teenage virgins were given a video camera and asked to record their lives over a three-month period as they considered having sex for the first time. They all express nervousness to varying degrees; they're all uncomfortable; all psyching themselves up for their 'big day' as if this were a first job. All quite happy to be filmed, model sexual negotiators, 'Giddens' Babes', democratic to a fault to whom the rest of us owe a debt of gratitude as they liberate us all from the patriarchal distortions of virtue.

Perhaps most 'gratifying' is the collusion of the parents:

Chervana, from Surrey was 'so ready to get it on' with a guy she dates, called Ant, but he stops returning her calls. 'I was going to lose my virginity to him,' she opines. 'Probably very ready to lose my virginity but there's something that's not ready. It's weird.' In desperation she turns to her mother, with whom she

---

9   Reich, *Listen, Little Man!* cited by Giddens in *The Transformation of Intimacy*, p. 162.

says she never usually discusses such matters. Mum offers sound advice: 'Why don't you wait until you are really sure?' she says. 'You need to be able to look back and think that was "right".'

Later, she tells her mum and sister she thinks she might be gay. Both accept this, although her mother suggests that it might just be a phase. 'My mum said "whatever makes you happy".'

Another participant, Craig, is filmed in his parents', house when they are out. He cooks his girlfriend Chloe an Italian dinner. The crew continues filming as he takes her upstairs to bed. Next morning, after successfully accomplishing his assignment, Craig invites the camera crew into the bedroom to film him triumphantly bringing Chloe a celebration breakfast. He says in his video diary: 'The film crew came round in the morning and I was like "yeahhh!"'

After a few weeks of 'mad rampant sex' (Craig's words) the couple are no longer an item. They discovered a significant difference. 'She's an absolute clean freak and did you see my room? It's a tip. That caused quite a lot of conflict and we went our separate ways.'

The Times carried a piece about this programme entitled 'Thrill of the chaste? Er, no'.[10] The reporter comments insouciantly, 'When I meet Chervana and Craig after filming is completed, I find two teenagers who, for all the sometimes glib statements that appear in the 22 minutes edited from their three months of footage, are bright, articulate and have thought a lot about their sexuality.' Well you would wouldn't you, if MTV were tagging your every erection. When one 17-year-old says, 'I really should have had it by now' and another says, 'Everyone I know has had sex . . . they are part of the "I've-had-sex"-gang. I want to be part of that. Be pretty cool', one can be sure that this pressure was not simply created by hormones. Three out of the ten lose their virginity by the end of the programme. We will never know whether possible participants

---

10   24 August 2006. The journalist was Damian Whitworth.

turned down a starring role in this drivel, or whether there are teenagers and parents out there with more sense.

The insouciance of the well-educated that passes for the 'democracy of the personal' is anything but. Judgements are being made all the time in a furious attempt to rid sex of its constraints. There can be no other civilization in history that turned this most fundamental of all rites of passage – the onset of sexual maturity – into a spectator sport; and did not hedge it about carefully with the symbolic rituals of acceptance into the group. For adults proactively to collude in the destruction of the means of future bonding, the act that more than any other knits couples, families and ultimately society together, is indicative of a kind of cult of mass suicide. In no society have children ever been groomed to regard sex as merely a lark, an activity unconnected to everything society holds dear; a kind of extreme sport they can negotiate alone. One day, the Chervanas and Craigs of this world may find themselves angry beyond bearing. They will rage at the duplicity and deception of their moral guardians who sold them for a sop. Against whom will they wreak their revenge – for those guardians will be long dead?

The huge propaganda exercise to take the pain and responsibility out of sex, by destroying social taboos and subverting moral discourse, is making teenage and other rape harder to prosecute, just as it is on the increase as a phenomenon. A girl's lack of sexual experience, which might once have been presumed, would make her claim of rape more plausible. But now, government is having to draft legislation to limit sexual history evidence in rape trials at all, as it – quite reasonably – weakens the prosecution case in an increasingly fraught arena in which the conviction rate has plummeted.[11] Where 33 per cent of reported cases resulted in

---

11 Home Office Online Report 20/06 – Section 41–43 of the Youth Justice and Criminal Evidence Act 1999 by Liz Kelly et al. 'Few young people or adults in the twenty-first century have had only one sexual partner. The majority of the population, therefore, has a "sexual history". Yet these sexual experiences can take on additional and negative meanings when introduced as "evidence" in sexual offence trials . . . No sexual history evidence should now be admitted, or questions by the defence allowed, unless a judge has ruled that they lie within one or more of four exceptions' (p. v).

convictions in 1977, the figure in a sample of 676 cases from eight police forces studied for the Home Office in 2003–04 had dropped to around 5.29 per cent.[12] This figure masks even bleaker facts, recorded by Walby and Allen in 2004, based on the 2002 British Crime Survey that estimated that in 2001 there had been 190,000 incidents of serious sexual assault, and an estimated 47,000 female victims of rape or attempted rape – the majority lost to the legal process.

Globalization too is having an effect on the safety of girls. The increase in women trafficked into the UK for sex is not the only problem facing police. Asian networks particularly are now abducting young girls for sexual exploitation after plying them with drink and drugs. Qaiser Naveed, 32, and Zulfqar Hussain, 46, from east Lancashire were sentenced to five years and eight months prison in August 2007 for abducting and sexually exploiting two girls, aged under 16, to whom they had given five and ten ecstasy tablets respectively at a motorway service station, before having sex with them. *The Times* and *Sunday Times* exposed the networks following the trial.

Christine Miles documented the girls' stories, and their families' struggles to be supported or receive justice, in a book entitled *Stop! She's My Daughter.*[13] Jessica Rogers was 13 when she was targeted and groomed by a network of Asian men. On numerous occasions, she was drugged and transported to several towns in the UK for sex before being dumped by the men. Once, she was left on the hard shoulder of a motorway in the early hours of the morning. Jessica was so heavily drugged, says Mrs Rogers, that she had absolutely no concept who she was. She told her mother: 'Mum, don't mess about: they'll come round here with baseball bats.'

---

12   London Metropolitan University, *A Gap or a Chasm*, 2005. This report revealed that rape conviction rates had reached an all-time low because of 'a culture of skepticism' among the police.
13   Available from CROP – the Coalition for the Removal of Pimping (0113 240 3040).

What is particularly worrying about the case is not just the age of the girls – they are groomed to have sex as soon as they turn 13, the age at which the state considers them adult enough to give testimony in court – but, in the words of Christine Miles – 'they are intimidated not to give evidence, and don't fully understand these men weren't real boyfriends.' There seems to be little cultural resistance enabling the girls to distinguish pimping from puppy love. The police have as yet no idea as to the extent of the problem, and there are no official statistics. The UK Human Trafficking Centre, which opened in October 2006, only has a remit to tackle trafficking of girls from abroad, and its website makes no mention of the local problem. Blackburn, in common with many northern towns, is experiencing a huge upsurge in pimping, and it is an unpalatable truth for the authorities – and indeed the police – that many of the newest wave of pimps come from within the Asian community, which often regards white girls as 'easy'. Research, conducted in 2005 and involving 106 families seeking help from the Leeds-based campaigning organization, Coalition for the Removal of Pimping (CROP), found that in Yorkshire alone more than 30 girls were sexually exploited, with some being forced into prostitution, by what CROP says are predominantly Asian networks.[14] As many as 200 families have gone to the organization for advice. Some despair of the police. Maureen, whose daughter Jo was one of Naveed and Hussain's victims, said: 'I was told by one police officer that he did not "want to start a race riot" by arresting Pakistani men for sexual offences". At the time of writing, the families were meeting lawyers to discuss possible action against the police, in what could result in the biggest civil action ever brought against police for failing to protect children from sexual predators.

Despite evidence from rigorous research by organizations such as the Home-Office funded agency CROP that the gangs are

---

14   This and other details, *Church Times*, 5 October 2007.

largely made up of men from the Pakistani Muslim communities, many are determined to downplay this. 'What we're dealing with is gross criminality,' says Aravinda Kosaraju. 'That should be confronted whatever the race of the perpetrator.' Nonetheless, according to Louise Brown, author of *Sex Slaves*, Asian attitudes to women and to sex right across the Asian world reveal the recent UK incidences to be the tip of an iceberg we've been able to ignore up to now, as 'foreign.' 'The trafficking of women for prostitution is a global phenomenon . . . it is [in Asia] however that the industry and trafficking networks are most sophisticated and well developed. Ironically – and astonishingly – it is also a part of the world in which the local men are thought not to buy sex,' she writes.[15] Hence its hiddenness. Globalization is just beginning to deposit white sex slavery on Britain's doorstep – and it is unlikely simply to go away, if society buries its head in the sand.

As the line blurs to oblivion between children's supposed right to sexual self-fulfilment (or not) and their vulnerability to gross sexual exploitation such as this, the Reichian vision, where parents and society actively encourage sex rather than protect their children from it by the reimposition of taboos and moral safeguards, is exposed for the nightmare it is. For it is only parents who, according to Christine Miles, can help address this problem. 'The true scope of in-country grooming and trafficking is currently hard to gauge. Piecing together parents' stories is the only way of gaining a clear picture of what is happening in the UK.'[16]

Parents, however, may be too busy 'protecting the love of their adolescent sons and daughters' – in Reich's chilling words – to protect their lives.

---

15   Louise Brown, *Sex Slaves*, p. 4. Brown adds that the extent of trafficking and abuse is inseparable from the level of sexual repression in society and the degree of control exercised over women. She singles out Pakistan: 'There is a beautifully neat symmetry: strict sexual codes and rigorously male-dominated societies are mirrored by widespread systems of sexual slavery and a regular supply of trafficked women to the sex trade.' Added to poverty and income disparities, the results are catastrophic for the most vulnerable (p. 25).

16   *Church Times*, 5 October 2007.

Chapter 4

Virtue and the Vamp: Women as Culture Carriers

The Pill, you might say, fell on fertile soil. Once the country had recovered from the war, translations of Freud's essay *Civilized Sexual Morality and Modern Nervous Illness* published in German in 1908 and followed 20 years later by the even darker *Civilization and Its Discontents* (1929) began to filter through into European universities and would provide the intellectual and moral justification for the profound changes implied by modern contraceptive science. With the Pill, sexuality, procreation and social responsibility – together the sources of neurosis as far as Freud was concerned – could now be separated. Marriage was no longer obligatory or even necessary. Sex was for pleasure, not for society. Disease, unwanted pregnancy and even the building of abiding families were now minor inconveniences that could be mechanically avoided or eradicated. Women at last were free. Any negative feelings they might have after sex were merely cultural residues, the result of a faulty socialization that could be re-engineered through psychoanalysis and changes in the law.[1]

1　The great march forward is still in progress. As I write, Anne Furedi, Chief Executive of the British Pregnancy and Advisory Service is insisting that only one doctor be required to agree to an abortion instead of two – a requirement she described as 'frankly arcane'. 'Having sex without repercussions is a right that should not be complicated by unwanted children', she said. This despite research carried out in 2006 in New Zealand that showed that women who had abortions suffered twice the level of mental health problems and three times the risk of major depression as other women, (*The Times*, 28 November 2006, p. 1, lead story).

This was a sociological revolution greater, according to some scholars, than anything since the end of feudalism.[2] It marked – theoretically – the end of any religious sanctioning of or even connection with sexuality. The rendering-irrelevant of the sacred to the secular – secularization – was most pronounced in the 'disenchantment' of sex; the attempt to render banal a sphere of human activity invested since time immemorial with sacred meaning. Callum Brown dates what he calls the 'death of Christian Britain' – and hence of that civilization associated with it – to 1963 and the invention of the Pill.[3]

In the 1800s, pious womanhood had been seen as the source of civilization. 'The problem is the man, sometimes the father, but more commonly the boyfriend, fiancé or husband, who is a drinker, gambler, keeps the 'bad company' of 'rough lads' and is commonly also a womaniser.'[4] Evangelicalism pietized femininity, in Brown's words, in order to help the reformation of society. 'Femininity became sacred and nothing but sacred . . . women's religiosity was critical to moral change in men.'[5] And Melanie Phillips notes how, by the end of the eighteenth century, the championing of private and domestic virtues had put women at the head of a movement of moral recovery. 'Women had become the guardians of morality.'[6] The 1894 novel *The Sacrifice of Catherine Ballard* gives searing insights into the brutality of gender relations in the Victorian period, which women fought so hard to overcome. A tale of colonialism, debt, a marriage of convenience and slavery gel topical issues of race, sex and human dignity in a single Christian perspective. 'Most powerfully, it presents women as the victim of male exploitation – of fathers who corrupt their daughters and destroy their lives for commercial gain, and of husbands drunk on

---

2   Duncan Dormor, *On Cohabitation*.
3   Callum Brown, *The Death of Christian Britain*.
4   Ibid., p. 77.
5   Ibid., p. 59.
6   Melanie Phillips, *The Ascent of Woman*, p. 5. 'Novels propagated this new ideology of femininity, associating sensibility with sympathy, compassion, benevolence, humanity and pity.'

power and an insecure masculinity expressed in racist denigration and extreme domestic violence. It is also about women's secret sacrifices, which may be hidden from good men, and known only to God'.[7] Illustrations from tracts echoed in the secular women's press indicate how integrated the evangelical discourse became throughout society as a whole.[8] The suffrage movement grew out of this kind of narrative – a narrative of feminine redemption that was sustained to a remarkable degree for the next 40 years until the Great War. Then things began to change. The prolific tract writer David Kyles told women in 1938 that it was the war which 'unleashed a pagan flood which swept away many a sacred sanction' and drove the nation into 'a remarkable surge of pleasure-seeking'. He wrote of a 'moral paralysis creeping over our people', in which 'women ceased to prize their womanhood'.[9]

This trend grew to become the norm. Today, the freed woman is discouraged from being pious or feminine, but 'sexually self-efficacious' and able to practise 'protection behaviour'. Sexual self-efficacy is defined as '[b]eing able to voice and enact one's own desires, interests and needs [which] is necessarily central to our conceptualization of sexual health', say three women researchers at San Fransisco State University, California.[10] Sexual self-efficacy is the second category of this investigation which is set within a 'feminist developmental framework' published in Canada in 2006. The research based on questions to 116 girls aged 16–19 found that 'internalizing conventional ideas about femininity was associated with diminished sexual health'. . . . 'Whereas traditional theories of human development had described the key tasks of adolescence

---

7. Brown, *Death of Christian Britain*, p. 77.
8. The reader is referred to Brown's comprehensive chapter on this, pp. 79–87.
9   D. Kyles, *Should a Girl Smoke: An Appeal to British Womanhood*, 1938, cited in Brown, *Death of Christian Britain*, p. 87.
10 E. Impett, D. Schooler, and Tolman D., 'To be seen and not heard: Femininity, ideology and adolescent girls' sexual health'. *Archives of Sexual Behaviour*, 35(2) April 2006, 131–44. This Canadian journal is the official publication of the International Academy of Sex Research.

as achieving separation and autonomy, for girls, in contrast, negotiating and maintaining close relationships mattered more' (what
is known as 'self-in-relation theory'). Negotiation of, and the desire
to maintain, changing relationships was a primary struggle in
adolescence for girls, according to the research. They found that
'[o]ne way in which girls and women maintained important relationships was to silence their own needs and desires as a strategy
to reduce conflict.' This the researchers call 'inauthenticity'. 'Girls
and women may be particularly vulnerable therefore to making
their own sexual needs and desires including the need for protection against STIs and unwanted pregnancy secondary to the
desires of their partners.' Femininity is the root issue. 'We suggest
that femininity may primarily inhibit girls' sexual self-efficacy,
which we define as a girl's conviction that she can act upon her
own sexual needs in a relationship such as enjoying sex, refusing
unwanted sex and insisting on the use of protection.' Femininity
they define as 'avoiding conflict, suppressing anger, being "nice"' –
and 'managing their own bodies and habits to conform with prevailing images of beauty and attractiveness.'

The conclusion that femininity leads to subjection or disease is
a long way from the pietized femininity of the eighteenth century
that led to social reform. By divesting ourselves of our femininity,
our need to be needed and our sense of a larger responsibility, we
can save ourselves and the rest can go to hell. When we have sex,
what we want is relationship. The answer is not to abstain from sex,
but to cease wanting relationship. That is ultimately what Giddens'
vision of the 'pure relationship' means – with everyone negotiating
a shopping list of 'satisfactions' they require to be met, ready to
bolt if they're not. Women are no longer 'subject to the phallus' to
use his delicate phrase. Now we must strive to liberate ourselves
from the complexities and unpredictability of desire too.

Science – evolutionism – still dominates this discourse; the
notion that 'progress' will one day rule out pain. But as Scruton says,
this is a fallacy. Desire is a function of institutions that constrain it.

No constraints, no desire and no love. 'No' is the most exciting word in the English language. When everything is possible, nothing is desirable. Dogs do not exercise desire, they simply mate. They do not dream, plan, long for the beloved to 'embody' them, write poetry, grow emotionally wise. Dogs copulate suddenly and violently, then run off to chase a stick. And nothing is required either to ensure it happens or ensure it does not – except neutering of course. But for humans, without the word 'no', sexual fulfilment itself vanishes. Without communities that are comprised of an endless equipoise of mutual constraints, individuality vanishes. True community implies difference. A group of identikit people is not a community, it is a regiment. And indeed, our communities *are* dying. Individualism has become uniformity. We all wear the same stuff – all that distinguishes young women from young men is their breasts; the (exposed) midriff declares 'vacant womb for rent – terms negotiable'.

The fight for a truly relational freedom – of self in communion – is a long way from being won as is clear from the literature of the past six decades. The dialectic between female misery and social structure has produced a huge literature, but Marilyn French's novel *The Women's Room* gives a seminal account. First published in 1977, it gives a graphic account of the struggle to find balance between freedom, self-fulfilment, love and sustainable communities emerging out of the stifling marital norm for post-war women. Mira's model marriage to the – aptly named – Norm ends not in divorce, but in her attempted suicide. The novel is not against marriage, but against *nuclear* marriage, a form of social organization that imprisoned couples in their own mutual fixation. 'We all learned to live emotionally alone', says Mira, the novel's authorial voice, sadly. The high water mark of this particular hell coincided with the corralling, in the US, of people into what were called 'neighbourhoods' – a metaphor for sociologically heterogeneous blocs: Latinos in Latin quarters, old people in homes, the insane in asylums, blacks in the ghetto. Those neighbourhoods didn't work – and neither did the marriages. 'The Italians hated the Irish and the Irish hated the Jews, and neighborhoods warred with each other.' But the breakdown of the 'hoods also meant the end of the extended family. That in turn meant 'too much pressure on the single family' and a huge question mark over the point or possibility of singledom. Val, the visionary, outlines her dream of true communities based partly on the hippy commune, partly on old Spanish towns clustered round their olive groves on timeworn hillsides, peopled according to a quota system to avoid ghettoism, where couples, singles and all other kinds of people live purposefully together.

In *The Women's Room* true communities are built around honest relationships where men and women have equal respect, and are accorded equal worth. The 'love' that was falsely idealized in women's magazines from the 1930s to the 1950s and also in much advertising was 'an insanity' created by 'the structure', Val claims. It was a false ideal reinforced by post-war austerity and faux-Christian disciplines in which women – and men – suffocated. 'There's been too much ought for us to find is', says Val. In the second half of the book, Mira, now on her own, goes to college as a mature student and falls in with a group of women who all in their various ways represent the ferment of social and sexual experimentation that characterized the post-Pill generation. All the women and the men whom they include in their group – the gate-keepers of this group are all women – are able to be completely open with each other, non-judgemental, supportive and loving. None of them is married – initially. Some are gay. Some get married. The novel decries conventional marriage for its own sake; it explores different forms of non-marital sexual intimacy and the various messes they lead to; it raves about friendship. Then Chris, the daughter of the feminist focus of the group, gets raped by a black kid. Male violence; the dysfunctionality of society's shadow; the impassable truth.

It is not a 'moral' book, but it is an important one since it portrayed so well the very real unhappiness from which the sexual revolution meant to release women. And it pointed to the serious fact that 'no woman is an island' – that to be whole we do not need A Man, but A Man in Community. Any serious recovery of chastity and hence of appropriate sexual desire can take place only in the light of lessons learned during those years. Sexual profligacy is not frivolous. It has deep roots in the darkness and despair of mental hospitals to which unmarried mothers were consigned, and in the eugenics movement born of imperialist white supremacism, for which controlled breeding was so important. And it has its roots in the enforced prostitution of rejected and outcast wives, as we will see in Chapter 7.

The Women's Room became a cult read among my generation of students anxious not to make the mistake of our mothers who had gone back to the domestic realm after the war, eschewing the education and independence the war had won for them. The suffragist movement had been endlessly frustrated, particularly by the intransigence of Prime Minister Asquith; but the First World War changed all that. 'Without the work of women it would have been impossible to win the war', said Churchill. And Asquith himself wrote to the suffrage campaigner Mrs Millient Fawcett on 7 May 1916 that he 'recognized the magnificent contribution that women were making to the war, and that in due course he would impartially consider the women's franchise'.[11] Women had run the country while their men folk were away at war.[12] In Whitehall, 162,000 women were employed in new ministries. They worked in the munitions factories, stoked furnaces, unloaded coal wagons and built ships. Although the Red Cross rejected women in 1914,

---

11 Phillips, *The Ascent of Woman*, p. 297.
12 Single women had also been setting up and running mission hospitals and schools in remote regions of the Empire since the 1860s – well before they were allowed to practise medicine in Britain, or to vote.

nonetheless two of the earliest women doctors set up field hospitals in France and then in London. But after the war, no one wanted to remember all that. An 'act of cultural amnesia' found women skivvying all over again. Perhaps everyone wanted things to be 'normal' again after the huge disruptions of a second war. Perhaps with families shattered or traumatized, they yearned for the stability of the 1930s when life seemed hopeful and calm. But this time there were no servants to mitigate domestic drudgery, and none of the old moral and social certainties. The renewed subjection of women is illustrated by a cutting from *Housekeeping Monthly* for 1951 – all the more startling given the heroic labours of women in the wars:

The Good Wife's Guide
Have dinner ready. Plan ahead, even the night before, to have a delicious meal ready for his return.

Prepare yourself. Touch up your make-up, put a ribbon in your hair and be fresh-looking.

Prepare the children. Take a few minutes to wash the children's hands and faces. They are little treasures and he would like to see them playing their part.

Listen to him. Let him talk first – remember his topics of conversation are more important than yours.

Don't complain if he's late for dinner or even if he stays out all night. Count this as minor compared to what he might have gone through that day.

A good wife always knows her place.[13]

At the same time, American businesses in the 1950s and even 1960s were marketing their goods to housewives with slogans like

---

13   *Housekeeping Monthly*, 13 May 1951.

'You mean a woman can open it . . . ?' to sell ketchup; or 'Get your husband to buy a new car . . . with the Selective Automatic Monumatic'; or even the astonishing 'Is it always illegal to kill a woman'? – to sell the Pitney Bowes postage metre to a boss enraged by his dizzy clerical assistant's ineptitude. Yet another depicts a [glamorous] woman lying over her husband's suited knee while he spanks her. The caption says: 'if he discovers you're still taking chances on getting flat, stale coffee . . . woe be unto you!'[14]

Too many women were too bamboozled by all this to escape the trap they'd voluntarily put themselves back into – as Marilyn French so clearly illustrates. It was left to my generation to take advantage of the circumstances that signalled the end of our captivity – and we did not need to wait to think what else we might be losing too.

We inherited our mothers' anger – and focused it. We knew things could not stay the same. We would liberate ourselves by using our minds. We would understand what had enslaved our mothers. Behind us lay the wreckage of the lives of so many bored housewives; women I met as a young reporter on the new housing estates of Thamesdown who were dying literally of apathy, of soullessness. Women like my mother who gave up her job to marry at 19, had four children by the time she was 25, never learned to drive, had no income of her own and was a supplicant for meagre 'housekeeping' money in her own home – and who killed herself with a cocktail of tablets her various psychiatrists made little effort to coordinate.

Freedom for us was a life or death issue; sex had become political. Freedom at almost any price was now our religion of salvation – and its high priestess was Germaine Greer.

---

14   *'You mean a woman can open it . . .?' The Woman's Place in the Classic Age of Advertising* (Prion Books, 1999).

Greer and the metaphysical woman

Greer came to town and lectured in a massive hall which did not dwarf her. She was large, loud, erudite and beautiful – and above all she was angry. It was exhilarating. She seemed to grasp all at once the lost potential of a generation of women who had meekly gone back to their ironing boards after the war, as if their meaning as creatures had always been to serve men. Never having been married, we, aged 18, could not have been authentically angry – but, curiously, our joy at hearing Greer was real enough.

My own mother seemed to have been invented just so Greer and French could write about her. She had given up her job as a secretary at the Metal Box Company in London's fashionable Regent Street in order to get married. She left the city with her rich new husband, fresh back from the colonies, only to find herself marooned in the countryside, away from all her habitual pastimes, and producing babies annually. She turned 21 in the maternity ward where I was born. Three more babies followed in quick succession. I remember her before she went mad – sad, wistful, totally lacking in confidence. In the village, her social life revolved around the Women's Institute: in her 20s! The subjects discussed were flower arranging, the perfect soufflé or some such thing. She never learned to drive. She had not needed to in the city. And she had never developed her mind. She had been courted by a rich ex-colonial administrator – but married a pauper who could never raise enough capital to buy himself off the smallholding he had come home from Africa to rent. She would buy new clothes they could not afford – and hide them. She would smoke Woodbines and not inhale. Her thrills came from betting a few shillings on the races she watched on telly, taking the tips from the *Jimmy Young Programme* on Radio 2, but only once ever actually summoning enough energy to attend a race meeting. And even then she lied to my father about where she was going. She wanted to be free, to be herself, and these pathetic little stabs at it only increased her guilt and frustration.

> The working girl who marries, works for a period after her marriage and retires to breed, is hardly equipped for the isolation of the nuclear household. Regardless of whether she enjoyed the menial work of typing or selling or waitressing or clerking, she at least had freedom of movement to a degree. Her horizon shrinks to the house, the shopping centre and the telly.[15]

The disarray of my mother's emotional life coincided with the dawning of a more general refusal by women to take it lying down any more. We can look to the last few decades as a time of sexual and moral chaos, a swamp of self-indulgence into which female intellectuals have led society. But why should women remain captive? Revolution destroys – but women were destroying themselves anyway. They had nothing to lose, in the famous Marxist phrase, except their chains. My mother committed suicide in 1979, three years after I graduated. She took an overdose of Mogadon tablets. In fact, she had been overdosing on pills for years. Doctors did not know she was taking 14 tablets a day of various mind-altering kinds: each one designed to compensate for the overreaction to the other. Greer sounded like the cavalry coming to women's rescue with her contempt for the *nuclear* family; her understanding of the isolation of women whether in town or country, and her take on the self-flattering delusions of the isolated and unsupported male who dominated them. Greer understood that sexuality was a social issue; that family is not for itself alone; that families implode, as mine did, unless they construe

---

15   Germaine Greer, *The Female Eunuch*, p. 224.

themselves as socially purposeful. And implode they have done. In the US, the most reliable figures show 41 per cent of marriages now end in divorce. In the UK and Europe the figure is slightly lower. Half of those who cohabit split within the first five years.[16]

In *The Female Eunuch* Greer describes the nuclear family as 'possibly the shortest-lived familial system ever developed.' She describes its antithesis, the *stem* family – exemplified or rather idealized from an experience of Tuscany – where the head was the oldest male parent, who ruled a number of sons and their wives and children.[17] The work of the household was divided according to the status of the female in question: the unmarried daughters did the washing and spinning and weaving, the breeding wives bred, the elder wives nursed and disciplined the children, and managed the cooking, the oldest wife supervised the smooth running of the whole.

Greer concludes: 'The isolation which makes the red-brick-villa household so neurotic did not exist'. She is right. Traditional villages in Suffolk where I grew up, were arranged around a green; houses looked in towards one another, where grandparents could watch the children playing, while the parents worked in the fields. My parental home, built in the 1930s, was one of 50 flimsy agricultural chalets in the middle of a field, built hurriedly by a government quango to resettle miners on the land after the war. Likewise, in the cities, grim Victorian terraces built on geometric grids also militate against sociality. Both were a convenient – and disastrous – rationalization. And inside those regimented cages, '[s]ingle eye-to-eye confrontation of the isolated spouses' has replaced the life of the tribe and stem village, where cousins play and work together and grandfather stalks the vine rows with his grandson on his arm.

---

16   *Breakdown Britain* (The Centre for Social Justice, 2007).
17   Curious that both Greer and French idealized a patriarchal form of social organization modelled in Catholic Europe.

Capitalism, education, urbanization and huge social mobility put paid to forms of social life underpinned by the stem family, leaving the 1970s husband and wife to 'dance the dance of diurnal murder', as Greer puts it. 'The father-protector, unable to assume any other field of superiority or prowess, was principally moral arbiter although unfitted for the role: the wife was a designing doll, disillusioned about her husband, confused and embittered by her own idleness and insignificance'.[18] Easier divorce was advocated because marriages became so torturous. Even the church changed its historic tune on divorce, and writers like Hugh Montefiore and Jack Dominian sought ways of softening the traditional ethic.

Germaine and the other prophets of the 1970s' social deconstruction were unhappy women as she admits. In outlining her dream of an Italian commune, she lambasts the myth of the *broken home* – the source of so many ills, and 'yet the unbroken home which ought to have broken is an even greater source of tension as I can attest from bitter experience', says Greer:

> The rambling organic structure of my ersatz household would have the advantage of being an unbreakable home in that it did not rest on the frail shoulders of two bewildered individuals trying to apply a contradictory blueprint.[19]

Greer's unhappiness became rage which aggrandized itself as a template, a philosophy – and drove thousands of us towards promiscuity and a different kind of isolation. Sex was now a political act without issue. Intellectuals did not want or expect to marry. We expected to live self-authenticating lives of our own, and if men were a part of those lives, they were so as adjuncts, not rulers. They were there – and remained there – by our choice. Unwarned about the aftermath of passion, unschooled in emotional self-protection,

18   Greer, *The Female Eunuch*, p. 223.
19   Ibid., p. 236.

unrealistic about everything awaiting us outside the university cloister, we drank up Greer's nostrums in the heady belief that we could refashion our world any way we wished. We at least had a reason for our madness, or thought we did. There was a moral in our immorality – the moral of self-preservation. We would break out – even if we did not know whither.

Greer recognized she was sending her aspirants into unknown territory, inviting chaos, anarchy and eventually the death of the state. She hinted irresistibly that promiscuity was better, even nobler, than exclusive dependency and neurotic symbiosis. She admitted she had invented a 'metaphysical woman' – one who did not exist – and set her up as an illusory goal upon an ever-receding horizon. She hoped 'the most successful feminine parasites would find her book offensive' – and called for subversion of the system that created them. Women were already lost; in the journey ahead they might begin to discover a will to live, a sense of what they wanted. Thirty years on, the power in her words still rings clear – but it does so across the wreckage of ruined marriages, pregnant children and rampant STDs. The horizon is no nearer. Women are no happier. Promiscuity is not the panacea for patriarchy and Helen Fielding's creation, Bridget Jones, hymns the death of a fantasy of freedom that made Greer famous.

Bridget Jones's Diary

The *Diary* first published in 1996 was a publishing phenomenon, one of the top-selling books, videos and DVDs of the twentieth century.[20] It chronicles the misery and squalor of sexually incontinent singledom. Helen Fielding's 30-something diarist survives in a feverish state of sexual opportunism – heightened by nicotine, alcohol and obsessive eating in desperate hope of rescue by a

---

20   Helen Fielding, *Bridget Jones's Diary* (new edn, Picador, 2001).

suitable mate. She struggles in vain for 'inner poise'. She tries out different imaginary scenarios in which her solitary persona might find its place. She lies. She self-deludes. On her birthday she decides she

> cannot be arsed to cook and would rather dress up and be taken to posh restaurant by sex-god with enormous gold credit card. Instead am going to think of my friends as a huge, warm, African, or possibly Turkish, family.

She decides to cook shepherd's pie for what will be 'a marvellous, warm, third-World-style ethnic family party'. Then in a flash, the homely self-image where 'love is what matters' changes to 'expect to become known as brilliant cook and hostess.' At the end of a disastrous spell in the kitchen, the friends arrive and sweep her off to a restaurant. Her final thought: 'Love the friends, better than extended Turkish family in weird headscarves any day.' What Bridget longs for – and actually has – is community, affirmation and forgiveness: an *urban* family, or as gay Tom puts it: 'We have extended families in the form of friends connected by telephone.' But the razzmatazz of urban culture, the need to stand for something as a beleaguered singleton, constantly lure her into false positions that turn out to be deceptive and degrading. Although she has sex with boss Daniel, it is because she imagines this is a lasting relationship, preparatory to marriage. She does *not* have casual sex with the delicious 23-year-old Gav whom Tom fixes her up with so that she has a partner for a dinner party with the Smug Marrieds. But it is vanity rather than morality that saves her:

> Eventually he managed to slide his hand over my stomach at which point he said – it was so humiliating – 'Mmm. You're all squashy'. I couldn't go on with it after that. Oh God. It's no good. I am too old and will have to give up, teach religious knowledge in a girls' school and move in with the hockey teacher.

Bridget has only the residual morality of her class – which not even her religious mother has managed to maintain by the end of the book. What saves her is not her own moral strength – but the man of her dreams. Fielding falls back on the Mills and Boon formula. For all her chaotic trendiness, Bridget Jones is deeply conservative, and utterly unlikely to be any kind of role-model for young women seeking hope from the suffering imposed on singletons by the increasingly illusory – but more aggressively peddled than ever – 'couple culture'.

Mr Darcy is without doubt a good man, as indeed is her father. Both are self-deprecating, quietly spoken, decent, bourgeois, self-sacrificing, generous. They both offer a love that accepts, forgives and ennobles – Christian love in fact. They both offer respite, res-cue, a *reason* to live. Though Fielding pushes the Jones character into real suffering – Christmas finds her 'totally alone' and there is no last minute bang on the door from a friend armed with cham-pagne and condoms – the book works on the premise that chas-tity is a temporary affliction, rather than a means to moral growth. Stigmatic, the mark of the outcast, better only than 'having an adulterous, sexually incontinent husband', as the unhappily married friend Magda puts it; a source of frustration, humiliation – and eventual death when the Alsatian finally eats you in your lonely bedsit.

> I sat, head down, quivering furiously at their inferences of female sell-by dates and life as game of musical chairs where girls without a chair/man when the music stops/they pass thirty are 'out'.

Bridget Jones has no horizon beyond self-gratification. Her obses-sion is herself – her weight, her status. She does nothing for the wider world, beyond observe its passing in a fashionable funk of smoke and alcohol. She self-reflects, but not to any higher purpose. She remains a child, and her ideal man remains her father. Her social function is nil.

Singleness a feminist issue today?

We have become blind to the way sexuality affects society – and society in return limits the choices we have. You learn to love what you know as Azar Nafisi points out in her novel, published in English in 2003, *Reading Lolita in Tehran*. The book, which takes its title from Vladimir Nabokov's deeply serious but often controversial novel, centres around an underground English literature seminar given by a disillusioned former teacher from the University of Tehran in the 1970s. Together they read excitingly illicit books, such as *Jane Eyre* and *Wuthering Heights*! They read American classics, and through them experience new horizons of metaphor and possibility. Nabokov's novel, *Lolita*, is pivotal in their self-understanding as intelligent Muslim women captive in a perverse political system. Thirteen-year-old Lolita, whom the paedophile Humbert Humbert kidnaps, comes to love the old devil, and even colludes with him in the satisfaction of his desire. When she does in the end manage to free herself, she opts for prosaic conformity in a mediocre marriage. Nabokov is a pessimist. Nafisi draws a parallel with the Iranian regime of the Ayatollahs, where people grow used to their captivity and adopt strategies of survival that they call happiness – or they commit suicide. Some escape to the West, but their new freedom is a very ambivalent one. It is not as they thought. For Nafisi, the fantasy, fed by the Christian values of nineteenth-century literature, gives hope – but in reality, the contemporary West offers only another form of subjection. Women are everywhere trying to invent a world that will not smother, enslave, humiliate or abandon them. The female self and society are intimately connected.

Right at the end of French's *The Women's Room*, Mira gives up on love because 'it meant giving up on everything else'. Even 'the consolation that love brought to the terribleness of life' is exchanged for the right to speak her own desires and decide her own fate, even when that fate means, as it must for a woman without community or faith, isolation and ultimately madness.

For French, the truth of the female self is a need for selfhood and love that cannot be realized.[21] The sacrifices love demands seem to be utterly one-sided. The woman, because she is smaller and weaker, is 'under' the man who makes decisions that take her complicity for granted. On the last page of the book, alone on an empty beach, marginalized, ageing and unemployable, Mira concludes: 'Forget: *lethe*: the opposite of truth.' It is a sad book and a terrible end. And yet it is full of brave experiments in love, an angry hopeful idealism that ultimately gives way to the narcosis [stet] Freud identified in women a hundred years earlier. And now? Thirty years on, the sexual freedom women have achieved has little to do with love or even pleasure. As one young informant tells Ariel Levy in *Female Chauvinist Pigs*: 'Sex is something you do to fit in.'

The twin traps of brittle, imploding marriages or the sex-obsessed restlessness of meaningless singledom are the potentially fatal options that secularism has offered. Yet there is another way, and single women are now freer than ever in history to seize it. We can liberate and use our sexuality to help refocus public morale and recover mutually loving and reinforcing communities. Chastity for the sake of ourselves and others is potentially the only way to generate that elusive matrix of self-fulfilling freedom-in-community. The historic connection between spirituality and sexuality – which we now go on to consider – can no longer be dismissed simply as patriarchal oppression. As we said once, we had that trip.

---

21   The mutually fulfilling complementarity and freedom for which French seems to yearn is, in Hebrew and Christian terms, a pre-Fall phenomenon. Patterns of domination and dependence that the Women's Room critiques is, in Christian thinking, not irreversible.

Chapter 5

The Church's Turn Against Chastity

It seems to me that, as far as Christianity is concerned, the changes in marriage and marital breakdown have to become an urgent priority, eclipsing all other social issues . . . marriage and the family are the root of society and the Church, and when they are in distress everything suffers in consequence. All we do is spend money and resources to look after disturbed children in schools and clinics, sick people in surgeries, delinquents in court, build more abodes to house the divorced couple, spend billions to ward off economic distress and, above all, create a vicious circle in which the divorced children of today are the divorced parents of tomorrow. It is astonishing how little importance has been paid by church leaders, with few exceptions, to this issue. The silence has been incomprehensible.

Jack Dominian[1]

Sexuality and spirituality are deeply interconnected. Control of the sexual body, from time immemorial the key to social development, political order and personal maturity, has been a religious prerogative. Herbert Richardson, Professor of Religious Studies

---

1   Jack Dominian and Hugh Montefiore, *God, Sex and Love* (SCM, 1989). It is still the case.

at the University of Toronto, in his analysis *Nun, Witch, Playmate: The Americanization of Sex* writes that '[s]ex is not some peripheral human function, but is the fundamental manifestation of the human spirit.'[2] How sexuality is managed is a deeply religious issue, integral to the religious activity of world-building. Christian tradition recognizes this. Chastity, according to this tradition, 'indicates a will unpolluted by self-interest or deceit, and directed firmly to the common good'.[3] The Thomist Patrick Riley says that chastity is linked to inner liberty, the 'perfection of the power to choose freely'. Roland Rolheiser says this perfection is violated when we experience anything irreverently or too soon. Chastity undergirds freedom; the perfection of free will is achieved through making the right choices habitually, without coercion, with reverence and at the appropriate time and place. Guilt in the refined individual conscience is a recognition of obligatedness. Its counterpart is gift. Guilt helps protect society, but in the knowledge that society will then be able to offer up willingly its goods in return. Self-control obviates the necessity for 'morality police'. It sets its own boundaries mutually. If society is viewed as a construct, a political and social reality, the pursuit of chastity is bound to be controversial. This is not the place for a prolonged review, but a few observations offered as a counterweight to the kind of writings we have surveyed in earlier chapters are warranted.

One must begin by asking the old question, What is society? A working Christian definition for our purposes might be that society is 'a group of men [and women] brought together in a relation of order established for a common purpose . . . A society remains in existence only when the intention to pursue and achieve a common aim is maintained, and provided that human misbehaviour does not mortally weaken the society.'[4]

---

2   Herbert Richardson, *Nun, Witch, Playmate: The Americanization of Sex*, p. 3.
3   Patrick Riley, *Civilizing Sex. On Chastity and the Common Good*, p. xiii.
4   Ibid., p. 17.

Society may be an accident in that one is born into it, but it requires human will to maintain.

What is the common aim of this group? The very being of that society. The well-being of society redounds to the well-being of each member. The well-being of each depends therefore on the society, civil and familial, in which we live. No one is an island – though we have learned to be peculiarly ungrateful for that fact, living as if we were uniquely the agents of our own destiny and survivability. Aquinas believed the purpose of society was to enable men and women to attain the good life, which included the moral life. What was society, he asked? A union of love. And what promoted that union? Ultimate ends and proximate ends. The only absolutely ultimate end was God.

> Men are united among themselves only in what is common among them. And this, most greatly, is God.[5]

The absolutely ultimate end of the universe was the glory of God, which was achieved through the maintenance of the order he put into the world in creating it. '[T]he greatest good in created things is the good of the order of the universe.' The proximate end was the well-being of persons – which explained the sacrifices people were prepared to make, believed Aquinas.

How you construe the ultimate end will determine what kind of society you have, and what you decide to put into it yourself. The sociologist Peter Berger says firmly that '[e]very society is an enterprise of world-building. Religion occupies a distinctive place in this enterprise.'[6] For sociologists, society is a product of man. 'It has no other being except that which is bestowed upon it by human activity and consciousness.'[7] Religion is of immense social

---

5   St Thomas Aquinas, *II Thessalonicenses*, III. 2
6   Peter Berger, *The Sacred Canopy*, p. 3.
7   Ibid.

importance, in that it informs our intentions and actions, which then act back upon us, shaping our possibilities. What we believe to be the case about life results in real consequences for others and for ourselves. If we believe we have no beliefs, or that any beliefs we might hold have no real bearing on others, society will become at best incoherent, and at worst, self-destructive.

By far the most enduring and influential set of beliefs about society is the Decalogue, or Ten Commandments. Crucially, the Decalogue was not the product of a people, but formed that people. The people who came out of Egypt were a rabble. They were not exclusively Jews. The Jewish identity was formed over centuries out of the Mosaic revelation. The name 'Hebrew' derives from *habiru* and all that means is 'outsiders'. Exodus 12.38 speaks of 'people of various sorts' who came up out of Egypt (Num. 11.4). They were neither clan, nor tribe nor religion, but were a 'mixed multitude'. George Mendenhall makes the point that '[i]n the desert, as also in Egypt, the entire group had no status in any social community large enough to ensure their survival.' They were merely those who could no longer tolerate the enslavement and oppression that their lack of organization had resulted in.

The Covenant is essential not only for understanding the existence of the community itself, but also the interrelatedness of the different aspects of early Israel's social culture. The period of Moses and the Judges according to new historical, linguistic and archaeological evidence, shows that religion furnished the foundation for a unity far beyond anything that had existed before, and the Covenant appears to have been the only conceivable instrument through which that unity was brought about and expressed.[8] And yet this rabble became a people whose influence, over 3,000 years, fashioned a whole civilization. 'The Decalogue is Western civilization's most basic political document'.[9] It rests on

---

8   George Mendenhall, *The Tenth Generation: The Origins of the Biblical Tradition*, p. 16.
9   Riley, *Civilizing Sex*, p. 55.

the principle that moral law is the substance of civil law. The Decalogue is both the summary of moral law, and civil law combined. The Decalogue does not contain the whole of the law – lying and fraud for instance are not included – but each particular law in the following books of the Torah becomes a symbol for the general. Says Riley: 'All deceitful speech is attached to false witness, all unchastity to adultery, all fraud to theft.'[10] Insofar as the Decalogue puts family survival under God as central to the survival of the new nation, chastity is central to the Decalogue, because it is essential to the health and survival of the nation. Not the modern understanding of family as claustrophobic, isolated nuclear unit, but much more the biblical understanding of family as porous, socially integrated group in many different kinds of relationship with non-family members for mutual help and support.

What was divinely given and religiously understood was in fact civil in character. Even after the various diasporas, the law kept the mystical nation of Israel together. The Covenant created the nation of Israel, not vice versa – and as such was exceptional. It's been called 'the most successful foundation document in history'.[11] Israelite polity made of Western civilization an extension of itself . . . carried within the Gospel in the words of Christ who said:

I have not come to abolish the law and the Prophets, but to fulfil them. I tell you the truth, until heaven and earth disappear, not the smallest letter, not the least stroke of a pen, will by any means disappear from the Law until everything is accomplished. Anyone who breaks one of the least of these commandments *and teaches others to do the same* will be called least in the kingdom of heaven . . . unless your righteousness

10 Ibid., p. 97.
11 Ibid., p. 57.

surpasses that of the Pharisees and the teachers of the law, you will certainly not enter the kingdom of heaven.[12]

Israel was uniquely a new society founded where none had been before, a society based not in blood, but in historical experience and moral decision. And today, where this ancient writ of covenant does not run, there is no society or even community, in the true sense of the word, but only family, clan and tribe. The law permitted a new kind of society. And as Max Weber discussed in *The Protestant Ethic and the Spirit of Capitalism*, the church based upon that law made human association possible across social divides that had otherwise stymied creativity and innovation. The church was an institution that permitted in its numerous locations the relatively free mixing of people who were not kith and kin or even all-men or all-women, but co-equal Christians, albeit modestly arranged on different sides of church buildings, for whom 'the dividing wall had been destroyed.'[13] When the law itself becomes oppressive, losing the love that makes sense of it, society becomes once more merely an 'in-group', a life-denying cult. Clan politics today bedevil groups without the law of love. Self-serving purity laws that dictate group boundaries promote death, not life.[14]

The Decalogue outlawed three kinds of offence: those against the Creator, on whom all else depended; those against nature i.e. sorcery (which led repeatedly to orgiastic worship and child sacrifice);[15] and offences against the common good. As civil law,

---

12   Mt. 5.17–20. Emphasis added.
13   Eph. 2.14.
14   Cousin marriage, which is banned in 26 US states, is practised by 55 per cent of the British Pakistani community, resulting in a high degree of genetic disorders, according to Communities and Local Government Minister Phil Woolas MP. http://www.politics. co.uk/news/opinion-former-index/children-and-family/minister-warns-cousin-marriage-birth-defects-$1201067.htm
15   See for instance 2 Chron. 28.3; Lev. 20.2; 1 Kgs 11.33; Ezek. 20.25 and 31; and Ps. 106 passim. The prevalence of child sacrifice and its associations with fundamental social disorder explains the sacrificial 'eat my body' and 'drink my blood' communion ritual instituted by Christ, the Firstborn of God who became thereby the last sacrifice ever needed.

the Decalogue did not deal with intentions but with acts considered so injurious that society itself would be destroyed – and punished them with death. Adultery was one such sin – not just a sin
against the family therefore, but against society itself. Hence
the *implicit* importance of chastity, which is part and parcel of
honouring the marriage bed, a theme Jesus reinforced. Random
sexual activity is the default behaviour for those without an
explicit ideology or ethic.

A domestic, family-based sexual order is central to Jewish life.
Jewish society was based securely around the married household,
in which *shalom* implied stability, order – and the begetting
of children. Even today, this holds good. Melanie Phillips, the
columnist and a member of the Finchley Synagogue, says, 'the
procreative family is a command to Jews'. She is characteristically
apocalyptic when she adds: 'We are on the way to destroying
ourselves because we are becoming a society of singles. Without
committed family, we shall no longer be able to look after each
other.'[16] Individual and social heroism to the Jew means singleness of *heart* in the light of the impending judgement of God.
Spiritual ambition is captured in the image of Moses standing
alone with his God on the mountain, radiant and transfixed – but
only for 40 days before he returns to his wives and flocks. There
was an alternative model, but it was only for the prophets. Ascetic
figures, whose prophetic calling had long been associated, in
Jewish folklore, with sexual abstinence, continued to emerge from
the desert to preach repentance to the nearby cities. The fact that
Jesus himself had not married by the age of 30 occasioned no
comment. It was almost a century before any of his followers
claimed to base their own celibacy on his example. At the time,
the prophetic role of Jesus, not his continence, held the centre of
attention. His celibacy was an unremarkable adjunct of his prophet's calling. Singleness was a badge of prophethood, respected as

---

16   Conversation with the author.

a sign of God's Kingdom breaking in upon and unsettling the everyday, domestic world.

St Paul dramatically developed the idea of singleness as being the better state. 'It is good for a man not to marry' (1 Cor. 7.1) and 'Now to the unmarried and the widows I say: It is good for them to stay unmarried, as I am' (1 Cor. 7.8). His noted preference for singleness raised the whole Christian community to the status of prophethood. By calling the body 'the temple of the Holy Spirit' he was rendering the earthly body a fit place for divine encounter, in terms of both presence, awareness and challenge. Sex was not out of place in this body – far from it. 'If they cannot control themselves, they should marry, for it is better to marry than to burn.' But the Kingdom of God was coming; the eschatological imperative meant it was not worthwhile marrying. Singleness and its viability remained – and remains – a *sign* of the Kingdom to come, and an encouragement that there is more to live for than the eye can see. It is a sign also of the dependability of God.

Where the Stoics had practised a very public form of abstinence to prove their manhood, believing sex with its emotional entailment was unmanly and contaminating, both Paul and later St Clement of Alexandria (AD 150–215), the first Christian scholar to devote a whole book to the subject, would have none of this.[17] 'Just as humility is a form of meekness and does not mean maltreating the body, so asceticism is a virtue of the soul practiced privately, not openly'.[18] Like Paul, Clement believed that human self-control was a gift of the Holy Spirit. Chastity which countered desire rather than integrating it altogether was mere exhibitionism. He cites the Brahmans, the holy men of India with whom the Greek world was familiar, whose 'hatred of the flesh', he believed, was 'ungrateful' and irrational.[19] He believed that

---

17   The third of his Miscellanies or *Stromata*.
18   *Stromateis* 3.48[3], in John Ferguson, *Stomateis: Books One to Three*, p. 286
19   Ibid., 3.60[1].

freedom from desire was a sign of the presence of the Holy Spirit for service.

> Human self-control (I am referring to the views of the Greek philosophers) professes to counter desire rather than minister to it, with a view to praxis. Our idea of self-control is freedom from desire.[20]

It was not enough simply not to eat, but not even to want to eat. Moses, he says, fasted for 40 days and 'felt no hunger or thirst'. 'We are children of will, not of desire', he says, citing 1 Jn 1.13, and only God could determine the will. He was not against marriage. Indeed 'celibacy is not particularly praiseworthy unless it arises through love of God' – a logical approach that applies to all appetite. 'Self-control means indifference to money, comfort, and property, a mind above spectacles, control of the tongue, mastery of evil thoughts.'[21]

Communal marriage was a feature contemporary with the early Church Fathers. Followers of Carpocrates and his son Epiphanes, for instance, who founded a heretic Christian sect on the island of Cephallenia to the west of Greece, regarded as righteousness that 'community and equity' shown in the animal world where 'God created everything for humanity in common. He brings the female to the male in common.' And, 'Everyone can share her as the rest of the animals show'. These heretical Christians used Gospel verses about 'holding all things in common' to justify orgies, the Christian 'love-feast' an opportunity to 'couple as they will with any woman they fancy'.[22] Such heresies degraded women and brought into disrepute even ordinary Christians, men and women who were otherwise able, through grace, to practise remarkable chaste fellowship, meeting together behind closed

---

20   *Stromateis* 3: 48[3]
21   *Stromateis* 3. 51[1], in Ferguson, p. 288.
22   Origen, *Against Celsus* 6.40.

doors. The behaviour of some in the church ruined by association the reputation of others. Even Plato's *Republic* is sanguine about group rape. While advocating a communism of the ruling class, where men and women had equal status, and neither possessed the other, he could nonetheless write, without a glimmer of irony: 'There is sexual abstinence and no promiscuity; copulation is permitted at festivals with a partner allocated by lot'![23]

Gradually the prophetic calling, made possible through sexual abstinence, was internalized by the early church. It made female ministry possible. Radical new Christian groups abandoned the settled Jewish life, and took to the open road to follow Christ, risking their respectability to live among brigands and the vagrant poor in the hills, preaching the Kingdom. Chastity permitted women to join the roving bands, ministering to those who had 'followed' Jesus, as they had once ministered to Jesus himself.[24] But for the most part Jesus had been perceived to be addressing the settled, decent married folk of the villages, exhorting singleness of heart, in the timeworn manner and idiom of the mendicant prophet. It was later that Christians began to identify Jesus not as a singular eccentric, but as the model for Everyman. He loved the married and the single, he exhorted faithfulness for all, but he modelled the unmarried variant of it, because the time was short, the demands of the Kingdom were urgent – and that Kingdom was imminent.

Christianity began to see itself as radical – and that radicalism meant risking the very survival of the secular social order in the pursuit of a greater goal. In times that were brutal and unpredictable, a small number of prominent Christian men and women used their bodies to mock continuity, through the drastic gesture of perpetual chastity. 'The means by which society was continued could be abandoned. Chastity announced the imminent approach of a "new creation." '[25] Early Christian treatises on virginity were

---

23   *Republic* 5.457 D.
24   Peter Brown, *The Body and Society*, p. 43.
25   Ibid., p. 64.

as earthly as they were heavenly, addressing publicly the physical agony of the married woman, and what Brown describes as 'the huge pain that any underdeveloped society places on the bodies of its fertile women' . . . 'their danger in childbirth, on the pain in their breasts during suckling, on their exposure to children's infections, on the terrible shame of infertility, and on the humiliation of being replaced by servants in their husbands' affections: "and all this they endure, seeing no end to their labors." Had they not married "they would be blessed, even if there were no Kingdom of Heaven for them to receive." '[26] Sixty years after Jesus's death 'the story of his resurrection from the dead and ascension into heaven became indissolubly linked with the shaking of the grip of death on all human beings, and, so, with a stunning suspension of the inflexible laws of the normal.'[27] Society's constraints and demands were not to be made a fetish of, for God might speak to any and all individually. God's purposes could not be reduced to one particular social form. Yet this was not a recipe for wild-eyed zealotry. The calling was to be lived out as a form of service, not as a form of mere enlightenment or self-perfection in the Eastern fashion. The dialectic of the Christian life, the life-lived-for-others, was its – and the community's – saving grace.

The socialization of sex

Sex and its painful, slowly evolving socialization have largely driven human development.[28] The socialization of sex has been able to take humanity from the prehistoric stage where it mimicked nature without constraints, through the monastic and romantic revolutions with their imposition of degrees of sexual delimitation,

---

26   Ibid., p. 25, citing Eusebius of Emesa, *Sermon* 6.5.
27   Ibid., p. 44
28   I am indebted to Herbert Richardson for this section. See his *Nun, Witch, Playmate: The Americanization of Sex.*

to the present age of sexual self-consciousness. We can do no more than glance here at a history of Western sexuality, and how chastity acted upon the shape it took and the effects of that.

Richardson argues thus: Once upon a time, sex was universalized and indiscriminate. Everything was sex, because life seemed to depend on it, and orgiastic human sacrifice was practised to appease its massive forces. All pre-Christian societies practise orgiastic human sacrifice. The Old Testament marks the beginning of this phase with its constant hints at the terrifying world from which the patriarchs led the people. The prophetic literature and the psalms constantly sound the alarm against indiscriminate sex, and the sacrifice of children (in the case of the Near and Middle East, sacrifice was to Molech) that always accompanies the sense of terror lying behind the visible undifferentiated world. (For evidence of this, see footnote 15.)

The Axial period, as this is known, which gave rise to all the great religions, marked the dawning sense of a world of change that was not explainable in terms of itself. It began to be apparent that there was an unchanging world of Reason beyond the sensory. This was not qualified or limited by death, and did not need appeasing. The monasteries grew out of the discovery that 'man's reason is his capacity not to will, but to know in a theoretical or purely contemplative way'. Rational consciousness universalizes – viz the brotherhood of Man, the Holy Catholic Church, the Muslim *Ummah*. Man's individual ego is no longer of first importance. But only in Christianity per se does he sacrifice his sexual life, discerning through his now freed spirit just what this sacrifice permits: that in order that the new man, and the new social community that seems to express his rational consciousness may come into being, he renounces sexual intercourse. The commitment to perpetual virginity meant that men – and women – now loved in a different way and for different ends. The purpose of this love ceased to be sexual orgasm and procreation – the establishment of the family – and became *caritas*, the love of the soul in the body, or the Christian in and for the body politic.

As long as men and women think of themselves as bodies and in terms of biology, they will regard themselves as incomplete unless joined sexually. Friendship on the other hand becomes possible once this biological view is superseded – as it was in the monasteries. The soul in the body was already complete in the contemplation of Christ in the other. As Richardson explains, friendship is not the sexual completion of the humanity of one person by another. At its highest, in the Christian tradition, friendship is a moral and spiritual communion between two beings, longing for Christ and in each other finding a very real sign or icon of that completion promised in the life to come.

Called 'Syneisaktism' in the early church, it meant that two people could live together as brother and sister. Those who experience this spiritual love know how freeing it is, and by how much it exceeds the joys of sexual intercourse. 'Frictionless flow' is what celibate married couples report that they particularly enjoy: a kind of surrender in love in which feelings of tenderness grow deeper – an increasingly deeper contact. One couple in Gabrielle Brown's *The New Celibacy* describe it as 'a subtle but permanent orgasm, not offset by fatigue or boredom'.[29] Such love may be completely infused with sexual feeling, but it has contained and sublimated the sexual urge. Feminists seek a way out from the sexual domination of men by demanding to be able to have sex *as* men. The spiritually mature know that spiritual love is better than sex because it releases one – not *from* the other – but *into* the other without possession, and therein lies the soul's true desire, and perhaps the greatest secret in a sexualized society.[30]

In his analysis of human needs as a hierarchy, Abraham Maslow found that genital abstinence characterized the most integrated, most self-actualized people functioning at the highest levels of

---

29   Brown, *The New Celibacy*, p. 22.
30   In an age of often spurious equalities, it is difficult to muster an adequate sense of the otherness of others, where discrimination has become one of the few remaining social sins.

human expression. What he found was that the individual's intellectual and emotional understanding and attitude towards celibacy was what made it healthy or not. He found that self-actualized people preferred sexual abstinence to sex without emotional or psychological commitment. (He also found that when they were sexual in marriage, they tended to enjoy it more intensely than others.)[31]

Indeed, the experience of this spiritual love between man and woman was so startling and so satisfying that for a thousand years the practice of perpetual virginity was chosen as the way to live and love. It formed the launch-pad of the civilization that emerged from the Dark Ages. Virginity was not the repudiation but the enhancement of love and the dignity of both man and woman. It did not deny sex, but retrieved it from genital fixation. It integrated sex fully back into the whole body and personality. Just as babies experience erotic love through their whole being, and genital awareness only comes as a stage on the way to full integration, so the same becomes possible between friends. Richardson suggests that this is ultimately the destination of all humanity.

He presses his point still further, through the eras of courtly and romantic love which gave way to the present age of self-consciousness. Courtly lovers, who were by definition not man and wife, and for whom the end was precisely not orgasm, destroyed the spontaneity of instinctual sexuality, and created thereby a new higher form of spiritualized psychological intimacy. It was expressed through Christian symbolism and metaphor. The sense of the 'beloved' was created through an intricate and prescribed system of idealization, which by symbolizing the sexual act and by linking every sexual act with a personal thought and intention, rendered whatever was done as more than merely the act itself. This deep psychological intimacy was created through conversation.

---

31   Cited in Brown, *The New Celibacy*, p. 170.

Man and woman were bound together in a union that was deeper and closer than the coital union of their bodies. It created a sense of narrative. The romantic period takes its name from the *roman*, the novel, when it became possible to view one's union with another as an ideal, a story, with a beginning, and a hoped for denouement. This union was itself symbolized through kissing (the organ of the soul), not through the genitals. And it elevated women, compensating for the ravages of the old domination.

The church and chastity today

The church, and the counselling industry it has spawned, have recently challenged this wisdom. Even in the monasteries, according to Kathleen Norris, counsellors 'contending against a strong cultural prejudice against celibacy' caution that emotional growth is doubtful in celibate relationships. To channel sexuality into anything besides genital activity is suspect.[32] Continence may still be an option in Catholic schools, and obligatory in seminaries, but the sex police make sure it gets a bad press. Gordon Thomas makes a strong case that continence is 'the guilt-ridden hangover of the attitudes that go with the severe patriarchalism of the Roman church'. By creating a separate, superior priestly caste, it becomes a self-defeating anachronism, he argues, 'leaving terrible scars in both women and men'.

He has popularized the anti-celibacy movement in his book titillatingly entitled *Trespass into Temptation*, written for the Protestant market. He seems to adopt the Freudian line when he writes that '[w]e cannot change our impulses – those urges that

---

32 Kathleen Norris, *The Cloister Walk*, p. 259. Norris is a secular journalist who was befriended by the monastic men and women who fascinated her, and went on to write the most unselfconsciously sympathetic and unembarrassed account of her various sojourns among them. Her book is highly recommended for its astonishing empathy and insights into the meaning and purpose of celibate life.

lurk in an unknown, inaccessible part of the subconscious. All we can do is learn to live with them through self-understanding.' He tells the story of one Father Philippe whose affair with Margot causes him to leave the church and marry, despite years of therapy provided by the Church, which 'diagnosed' him as 'at risk'. The terrible tension between his twin loves – for his vocation, 'the perfect ideal' and for Margot – leads him to claw unawares at his thighs at night, and draw blood even as he sleeps. He is prescribed drugs for stomach pains and headaches, and psychiatric help for 'soul pain' and ends up in the Chronical Dependency Unit. Convincing enough evidence, decides Thomas, for the view that sanity demands sex; that the celibate are unsexed, deluded or mad.

The widespread corruption of the celibate priesthood in America and all over the Catholic West, is seen as incontrovertible proof of the victory of sex over the spirit, rather than what it is: the outcome of an ideologically and commercially driven secularization that creates lonely, acquisitive and obsessional societies. Societies that squeeze out a sense of transcendence and destroy peace of mind make loners and eccentrics of Christians. Such societies feed parasitically, in commercial terms, off the compulsions they induce. Christ was never afraid to touch and be touched and himself moved freely in a mixed community of loving intimates, men and women. Yet today, priests must bear the huge burden of pain of our societies in often grim isolation. According to Richard Sipe who lectures and writes on celibacy for the Catholic Church, their formation and support are both inadequate. And society is witheringly judgemental of any lapse, paradoxically rendering it all the more likely. A lifelong process of sexual self-understanding is often short-changed from the start, by seminaries and students alike that expect too much too soon, or that idealize what's at stake.[33] The onslaught against purity – which

---

33   See A. W. Richard Sipe's wise and measured examination of the subject in *Living the Celibate Life: A Search for Models and Meaning*, especially pp. 39ff.

requires equanimity and supportive communities – is massive. Even the church is allowing itself to believe that sex has won. It is unrealistic in its demands on priests, which further compounds the difficulties of faithfulness.

It would appear that many in church leadership do not set their sexual or spiritual sights particularly high. Could it be that the church's failure to acknowledge the prophetic ministry in any meaningful way today, both compounds and is compounded by the sense of purposelessness felt by single people? True, there are communities of celibate men and women today, but their point is largely lost, misconstrued or gently mocked as a pious aberration, an escape, at best a special calling for the few – and certainly dying out. Robbie Coltrane, unforgettable in habit and wimple as 'Sister Euphemia of the Five Wounds' in the 1990 comic gangster movie set the amusing but irreverent tone. Celibates are marginal rather than central to the church's witness; in the current individualist idiom, they've made a 'lifestyle choice'. For the rest of us, a humdrum moral mediocrity may be all that is required. The church now teaches that sexual disorderliness is to be expected, as the young 'explore their sexuality'; or as the middle-aged 'cope with loneliness'.[34] It is necessary say Jack Dominian and Hugh Montefiore to be realistic in discussing sexual ethics. 'We must not dilute Christian ideals and Christian teaching. But we have to deal with actual situations in which human beings are called to act with integrity. Human well-being must be our goal, with real compassion for the unhappy. Personal moral qualities matter most. God has shown that love is more basic than law.'[35] But realism and compassion are at risk of obscuring and even denying the ultimately healing ideal. Once when I made a confession of a sexual sin to a priest, brave, fearful and expectantly longing in my heart for the restoration of absolution, he snorted at my priggish

---

34 Dominian and Montefiore, *God, Sex & Love*.
35 Ibid., p. 21.

self-righteousness and told me to get a life. I felt foolish, confused and angry and consoled myself with the belief that I had done what God required – even if the church no longer believed it. This same priest was later exposed – by his wife – to the church authorities for his affair with a male prostitute.

The church, far from proscribing sexual exploration or even certain kinds of sexuality, is now often indistinguishable from the rest of society on the subject of sex, and cohabitation has been endorsed by synod as an 'equally loving environment' for bringing up children.[36] The search for a livable accommodation between emotional need and sexual constraint for the sake of society is exercising the church, even while some within it appear to have renounced its traditional stance. A new approach to cohabitation seems to promise much, according to the Dean of St John's College, Cambridge, Duncan Dormor, but risks delivering just more confusion. He advises the church to 'get real' about sex before the church becomes irrelevant altogether. He writes:

> Rather than shouting from the edge of the pool then, like some authoritarian parent, advocating a 'deep end' theology of marriage, the Christian community could be 'up to its neck' sharing the genuine difficulties men and women face today and grounding the Church more securely in the everyday domestic world.[37]

He wrote *Just Cohabiting: the Church, Sex and Getting Married* in response to a sense that the church was merely 'fiddling in Bible land' while society burned, and was not facing up to reality. In 1995 a working party of the Church's Board of Social Responsibility

---

36 'Cohabiting couples and those in same-sex relationships can provide an equally loving environment in which to raise a child as married couples – and therefore should not be barred from receiving IVF treatment.' Report of Synod debate on IVF in *The Independent*, 26 November 1997.

37 Duncan Dormor, *Just Cohabiting*, p. 122.

had attempted to recognize new forms of family and had spoken somewhat cautiously of cohabitation as 'a step along the way' to marriage, while recognizing that 'the institution of marriage retains its centrality.' For Dormor, the case was not so cut-and-dried. Cohabitation was increasing because the rationale for marriage had collapsed over the last 30 years. While Christians might believe pre-marital sex was wrong, they no longer knew why. Sex for the church is about babies, asserts Dormor. With the advent of highly effective contraception this traditional cornerstone to sexual ethics, often obscured by the elaborate edifice which had been placed upon it, was removed. 'What we have witnessed in the last thirty years is the edifice of Christian sexual ethics teetering over the gap in its foundations.'[38] A more relaxed view based on sex as pleasure rather than procreation was surely in order. In which case, cohabitation should be viewed as one more stage in the development of relationship. 'If a period of living together before legal marriage came to be seen as a natural part of the process of becoming married, the marriage service itself could be more consciously reconceived to meet this reality, becoming an act of celebration and confirmation, rather than of registration and initiation', he writes.

For the couple, relationship is, he says, a fundamental dimension of everyday life, 'the primary place where the transcendent is encountered through the love of another' . . . which seems to beg the question. Becoming a couple at all is hardly more likely as marriage loses the sacred mystique associated with first intercourse. It is even less likely with the vicar snooping around hoping to 'opt in to this sphere of potential influence', as Dormor puts it. New liturgies for the unwed are unlikely to make the church itself more appealing, and their advocacy sounds like sanctioning cannabis just because so many people are dying of crack cocaine.

---

38   Ibid., p. 3

There have been other attempts to move the traditional goal-posts and welcome back pleasure as the theological cornerstone of the sexuality debate. The Archbishop of Canterbury waded into the debate while still at Oxford and his views on homosexual sex are well known in principle, if not in detail. He wrote then, in a lecture given in 1989 and subsequently republished three times, that 'sex forms persons', echoing Freud. He believed then that 'for my body to be the cause of joy, it must be there for someone else'. It must be

> perceived, accepted, nurtured: and that means being given over to the creation of joy in that other, because only as directed to the enjoyment, the happiness of the other does it become unreservedly lovable. To desire my joy is to desire the joy of the one I desire: my search for enjoyment through the bodily presence of another is a longing to be enjoyed in my body.[39]

He is surely right, and marriage is provided for just this. But he is overly sanguine about the devastation wreaked as we learn the lessons, and even without the essay's remarks on homosexuality, this would have been a controversial contribution to moral discourse. Anyone who discusses these dangers is 'overly anxious about sex', he suggests, and therefore, by inference, prurient, or immature. The grown-up rest may make their own lifestyle decisions.

> Decisions about sexual lifestyle, the ability to identify certain patterns as sterile, undeveloped or even corrupt, are . . . decisions about what we want our bodily life to say, how our

---

39   Rowan Williams. *The Body's Grace* (The 10th Michael Harding Memorial Address, 1989), p. 4.

bodies are to be brought in to the whole project of 'making human sense' for ourselves and each other.[40]

For the future Archbishop, then Lady Margaret Professor of Divinity at Oxford University and a trustee of The Institute for the Study of Christianity and Sexuality, sexuality is a matter of personal choice – exactly the opposite of what St Paul meant when he said 'You are not your own'.[41] *The Body's Grace* subtly and movingly explores the gamut of sexual love – but in a way that ultimately excludes not just the conventionally married, but those whose marriages are not sexually successful, and more especially those who must live in dignity without sex at all, through circumstance or choice.[42] Least included at all it seems to me are those who take the Bible at face value.

The essay begins with an exegesis of Paul Scott's *Raj Quartet*. Far from critiquing the irony of Sarah Layton's disgrace, Williams uses her postcoital sense of having 'entered her body's grace', as the foundation for his theological treatise. Like most men, there is a part of Williams' instinctual nature that assumes that any spinster who experiences sex will be thankful for it, no matter how beastly the encounter. It is precisely this attitude that encourages the less cultured mind to couple chastity with eccentricity, turn date rape into a sport and consign the Christian sex ethic to the dustbin.

Williams builds his own sexual ethic upon 'the processes of bodily desire and delight in their own right'. To be wanted is to be human as God intended. To be desired sexually, and to explore

---

40 *The Body's Grace*
41 1 Cor. 6.19.
42 I was surprised to hear that a married friend felt as excluded by this essay as I did myself. Indeed, I found myself in tears after reading the essay, and my response to it here comes after trying to understand the pain of my own involuntary reaction, rather than as a contribution to the discourse on homosexuality of which this essay was a part.

this desire, is to come close to the meaning of God in creation. In the novel, Sarah Layton comes out to India to stay with her mother and tries hard to live generously and authentically, despite feeling a misfit. She is seduced by the womanizing Clark, becomes pregnant and undergoes an abortion. According to Williams, she is – somewhat bizarrely – the better for this. He writes:

> Nothing in this drainingly painful novel . . . suggests that the moment of 'the body's grace' for Sarah was a deceit. Somehow she has been aware of what it was and was not: a frontier has been passed, and that has been and remains grace: a being present, even though this can mean knowing that the graced body is now more than ever a source of vulnerability.

Until then, Sarah 'is present fully to no one and nothing', says Williams. She represents a civilization that kept itself aloof from intimacy. Now the modern generation wants to engage, to be like everyone else; to end the difficult, laborious, effort of restraint and social improvement. But why engage in sex? Why not subject yourself to being hit over the head by a half-brick. It's the same body.

Williams seems to miss the point that the post-Raj generation that Sarah represents – eager, generous, outgoing – is nonetheless just as empty, alone and 'not present to life'. No longer able to live with the ambivalences of empire, nor yet able to connect with the emerging reality, Sarah, like England itself, simply falls prey to an ersatz 'love', a democratization of aspiration that in fact leaves her – and it – in chaos, degraded and doubly void. Scott's is a hopeless vision, because unredeemed by Christian hope. But Williams misses this. He construes Sarah's 'fall' as in fact hopeful, missing the irony of Scott's usage. The body's grace is *dis*-grace. After she is seduced by Clark, the 'void has been filled, she has experienced grace, and entered into some different kind of identity', says Williams. Actually it is nothing of the sort. Sarah remains empty – except for the bitter aftertaste of physical and emotional violation. She is forced to evacuate her womb, the price for evacuating her principles – for nothing. And England evacuates India – in a humiliating and hasty embrace of a new world order that is merely an absence of any kind of relatedness or mutual obligation; indifference, in a word.

With due respect to an essay rich in cultural allusion and deeply read, this is nonetheless surely a misreading of a state of mind that is more to do with spiritual and cultural bankruptcy than a search for identity. As Lord Devlin, former Master of the Rolls has written: 'History shows that the loosening of moral bonds is often the first stage of [social] disintegration' – which was Scott's point.[43] For Williams, however, in thrall to fashionable post-authoritarianism, even loveless sex bestows grace. It leads logically to his extraordinary view that 'rape, paedophilia, bestiality' are merely 'asymmetrical sexual practices' rather than the outrage they really are. He cites the philosopher Thomas Nagel who, he says:

> makes . . . a number of interesting observations on sexual encounters that either allow no 'exposed spontaneity' because they are bound to specific methods of sexual arousal – like sadomasochism – or permit only a limited awareness of the embodiment of the other because there is an unbalance in the relation such that the desire of the other for me is irrelevant or minimal – rape, paedophilia, bestiality. These asymmetrical sexual practices have some claim to be called perverse in that they leave one agent in effective control of the situation – one agent that is, who doesn't have to wait upon the desire of the other. (Incidentally, if this suggests that, in a great many cultural settings, the socially licensed norm of heterosexual

---

43   Patrick Devlin, *The Enforcement of Morals.*

intercourse is a 'perversion' – well, that is a perfectly serious suggestion.)[44]

Williams, eager to ingratiate himself with his unconventional audience, falls into his own trap of moral relativism. Conventional morality is actually the problem, he says; it absolves us from the difficulties we meet in deciding our sexual lifestyle, 'because the question of human meaning is not raised.' If God made us for physical rather than spiritual joy, then we have a *moral* duty to attempt the risky experience of 'the body's grace', he implies. Any attempt to avoid risk in sexual activity, rather than being commended as either common sense or biblical obedience, is dismissed as 'heterosexist' – and worse. The only 'perversion is sexual activity without risk ... Distorted sexuality is the effort to bring my happiness back under my control and to refuse to let my body be recreated by another person's perception.' Our very identity for Williams is being constructed in the relations of bodies. We belong with and to each other. There is *'no alternative to the discovery of the body's grace'* (italics mine). Those who withdraw their *sexual bodies* from the enterprise of human beings making sense in collaboration, in community – as indeed the biblically chaste have struggled to do for centuries – are the really distorted personalities. There is no other way to become a person than through sex. Their sexuality is more akin to the 'pathology of the torturer' (p. 6) than the prescriptions of the Torah.

Richard Kirker, Chief Executive of the Lesbian and Gay Christian Movement was 'astonished' in 2006 when Williams attempted to downplay this lecture. In an interview with a Dutch newspaper, Williams had said it 'did not generate much support'. Yet Kirker cites Williams' promotion to Archbishop of Canterbury (2002) 'in the full knowledge by the appointing bodies that he stood by the lecture' as evidence that the opposite was the case.

---

44   *The Body's Grace* p. 4f.

Even a *Sunday Telegraph* Poll of Anglicans in the pews in 2006 produced a majority in favour of having a partnered gay priest in the Vicarage, indicating the 'benign influence he has had up to now and how much of an inspiration 'The Body's Grace' will continue to be regardless (or because) of subsequent events.' Kirker adds that the Archbishop of Canterbury could not now pretend that the past 20 years had not seen a 'largely beneficial sea change in thinking on human sexuality issues and that he was, to his abiding credit, in the vanguard of this transformation.'[45]

45　Richard Kirker, 'The Body's Grace by Rowan Williams', 27 August 2006, http://www.lgcm. org.uk/html/AngText03.html

Chapter 6

Alone Again – Naturally

The road to God always begins in the sexual appetite.

St Bonaventure

'In the end it's just you. Alone.'[1] So says Russell Brand in his memoir, facing the fact of his sex addiction in a miserable treatment centre in Philadelphia. And so, on the face of it, it is. Sexual abstinence, like any other restraint, faces one with 'the actuality of life's solitary essence', as he puts it. For many, this is simply too terrifying. Many writers from Augustine[2] onwards are agreed there is a core sense of abandonment in each of us, stemming from who knows what? – our emergence from the womb? separation from our mother's breast? that is too radical to face alone. Without God, people seek to insulate themselves from this radical separateness in various ways and for too many, like Brand, they use sex. 'At the end of the day . . . there has to be some form of punctuation, or life just seems utterly relentless', he says. This book's aim is to encourage people not to 'insulate' themselves at all, but to have the courage to follow Christ into the unknown, comforted by his peace, turned outwards towards others, vulnerable yet always safe in his promise. Men and women of all ages and backgrounds

---

1 'I was in an orgy' *The Guardian*, 12 November, 2007 promoting his new book *My Booky Wook* .
2 'Thou hast made us O Lord for Thyself so that our hearts are restless til they rest in Thee.' *Confessions* (AD 397–8) I, i.

do bravely set off down the road of sexual abstinence in blind faith, and struggle to grow into their full selves, despite the cultural barrage that, as we have seen, either coerces them into sexual activity, or convinces them that any alternative is perverse.

What follows are stories that seek to explain why ordinary people, who struggle with their 'inner loneliness', nevertheless do not resort to casual sex. Some stories indicate a complete transcending of neediness; some do not – yet. All are moving – and all are instructive, pointing to a path that is its own reward. What becomes clear is that sexual abstinence is a process. It starts with a resolve, and may require much soul-searching, and even some slips. Abstinence may initially offer merely a shelter within which the hurt heart can find its own healing. It may require total submission to and trust in, an external Lover who can use it, like credit in the bank, for individual and social good; purposes it is not possible to foretell. This is true as much for single lay people as for vowed clergy and, lived faithfully, can lead to God, to tranquility – and to the recovery of community.[3]

The Christian divorcee

Cecil James is a 56-year-old security guard at the British Library, a job he's had for four years. A Sierra Leonean Krio educated at CMS Grammar School in Freetown, who fled his homeland during the war in 1994, he lives in Brixton and attends the Ruach Ministries Pentecostal church. It has a congregation of 4,000.

He had just attended a conference on 'Singles' and was delighted with the affirmation and encouragement it offered. So delighted was he that sight of my book as he checked it out – Aune's *Single Women: Challenge for the Churches* – caused him to light up and comment: 'There should be one called Single Men.'

---

3   Interviewees' names and locations have been changed to avoid identification.

I took him for coffee at Starbucks, over the road from the library, and sat, enjoying his melodic Krio intonations, his kindly way of saying Oooh yes, and nodding solemnly as he spoke. A tallish, gentle and earnest man, he was not the least bit fazed that he had had to remain chaste since 1991, when his marriage ended. Sex was for marriage, as far as he was concerned, and the right opportunity had not arisen to remarry. He was keen to press on me the three lessons from his 'Singles' conference:

- God has made certain people to be single forever.
- People will try to force you to get married just because you are single, but you can resist, because God has an 'assignment' for you.
- Not everybody will get married.

'I would love to be married as I am sitting here, but I always pray over anything I want to do. I pray that God will choose the right partner for me.

'I divorced my wife, because her late mother interfered. This is particularly so with Africans. I was married from 1972 to 1991, but I wanted to free my conscience. I fasted and prayed and God told me not to go back down that road, not to go back to her.

'Yes, I would marry again. But I would like to get somebody who would be mother and brother and sister and above all a best friend. Someone who I can pray with. Someone who would know when you are down and up, who knows when you don't have money.

'I was an Anglican. I used to go to St Charles [Church] in Regent. It has one of the oldest stone churches in the whole of Africa. They have just installed a new pipe organ.

'Both have advantages and disadvantages. Being more attached to the church – even in the Bible, it states there is nothing wrong with being single. Make no mistake about that. Maybe God ordained it for a purpose, for him to use you in his Kingdom.

'If I come to church at 8.30 I don't come back until 3pm. I am in the men's ministry, the prisons ministry. We do have a lot of single people. A lot of people go there to get married and some do meet their partner there, and they get married. I enjoy being single at the moment. I do what I want to do. I do my own cooking. I take solace. I read my Bible. I look at the God Channel on TV. I only get satellite because of the religious channels. I have my religious CDs. As far as loneliness goes, your own family thinks it's a taboo, and you can be a burden to them. I know the God I am serving so I don't care.

'Christmas Day is the hardest. And in case you fall ill there's nobody there. But I know the God I serve. He is not a God of failure – oh yes. At church, they tell us not to be too spiritual, i.e. don't *not* talk to somebody. But you should be a bit more relaxed. *Agape*[4] love. It doesn't mean if your brother sits near you, you should not talk to him. Agape love is there – oh yes. If someone is sick, the whole church will pray, oh yes.

'When you are single you are open to temptation. You have to get strength of character. That's why you must always read the Word. It's wrong to get into temptation because you will not be doing the will of God. Oh yes. It's possible. You have to get that will power. Adam and Eve had a choice and they chose evil. I used to smoke, but I gave it up 23 years ago.

'My conscience [*touching his heart*] – I do come across people I might like to marry . . . but I pray over it [*shaking his head*].

'There's a time for every purpose. You must pray over it.'

The Muslim divorcee

Roxana, 44, patrician, exotic, terribly overweight, is a 44-year-old Muslim from a former British Protectorate in the Pacific. In the

---

4 The Greek word used in the New Testament for the new kind of intense, total, empowering love the early Christians had for each other, derived from the love they had experienced in Christ. It has the intensity of sexual desire – as with God's longing for his creatures – but without the praxis.

alfresco bar of the British Library, where she is reading for her PhD, she tells me the story of her extraordinary, brave but unhappy life in the very upper echelon of one of the top Muslim families in the world. Her great grandfather on her mother's side was Ibrahim L, Attorney General of the islands until 1965 when the British withdrew. Her mother, aged 16, ran away from her father just after she was born and they took her to court to fight over her when she was 9 years old. She was brought up in her maternal grandfather's huge house – years she describes as 'the best of my life'. Her father was the son of the Chief of one of the southern atolls, who won a scholarship to study in the capital city, and became Director of Customs and Excise. Her ex-husband, one of the wealthiest men in the world, is a politician and brother-in-law to the wife of the President. Roxana comes from a long line of strong-willed women, and educated men – and combines both in a striking personality that is unconventional, sensitive but schooled to be tough. She has an immense, wistful dignity and has struggled to stay true to a confusing set of values that have been weighted against her.

Divorced after 16 years of loveless marriage within the presidential family, she still misses the warmth and closeness of family, of belonging. Her marriage represented a life of a kind, and gave her almost unequalled status. Yet it failed her emotionally and she dared to risk social and financial oblivion in order to be free and recover her self-esteem. She compensates with work – as a very senior official in the Ministry of Education – but is still 'yearning' for sex, companionship. She is, however, chaste. 'Sex should be within this box of marriage'. For her, marriage might even mean being a second wife; a 'part-time marriage', she calls it. She got used to having to share a man with numerous others as the wife of a rich Muslim politician, and would not mind the compromises again. She says she is 'prepared to choose the bits she wants.' It does not, on the face of it, bother her. This is chastity, Muslim-style – where men do as they please and women must stick to the sexual code no matter how much it loads the dice against any kind of emotional fulfilment. It all has a very Victorian ring to it – and Roxana is perhaps a Pacific-island Emmeline Pankhurst. Her place in the first family brought great honour but also huge responsibility, to be borne alone. She shouldered a remarkable career as a pioneer educator of women – but it was one that was foisted on her by dint of patronage. She was made President of the Women's Association at the age of 24, and later Principal of the premier girls' school in the country, named after the first President who introduced education for women. She was Deputy Commissioner for the Girl Guides, and Director of the Olympic Academy, taking the team to Barcelona for the 1998 Olympics. When I met her she was Director of a key department in the Ministry of Education, the Educational Development Centre, and was finishing her PhD at the Institute of Education at London University.

'There were 40 people in my house. At age 11, I was raped by one of the men in the house. At least I was made to have sex against my will. That was my first experience. Then I had a crush with a guy I allowed myself to kiss. I was about 14. I let him touch me and I liked that experience but I think my mother saw something developing and she stopped me seeing him. Again my lesson was, it's wrong. Then I had a boyfriend who lives in England and I saw him two days a year. We wrote long letters to each other. It was nice and innocent. My husband came along when I was 16. He penetrated my home, I would say. He was 15 years older than me, already married to my boyfriend's auntie. She was promised great gifts if she could convince me to talk to him. This man started coming and visiting and my mother was expecting me to be nice to him. You are allowed four wives depending on how much you can afford. He was an up and coming politician, a businessman, fairly established as a well-to-do person. My mother was quite adamant in allowing him into the house. After two years, he would come every single night. Eventually I said I would marry him. I was a virgin [no sense of contradiction or irony here, in view of her earlier mention of 'rape']. I liked him, I learned to love him, but I was like in a box.

'I really didn't know what it was to be made love to. Even now it hurts me. When we had sex, I would call it rather that he rammed into me. It was not in a way that I was allowed to participate in. He was boss. He knew what he wanted and he did what he wanted and I was just the instrument for his pleasure. The first time, because the pain was so sharp, I screamed my head off and that shocked him. He thought I was acting. The blood revolted him and he was put off me. I was put off him because he put me in so much pain. I was 18. I dropped out of 'A' Levels. That wasn't a very wonderful beginning I would say!

'I married as a second wife and he had no relationship with his other wife as far as I know. Over the days and months I allowed myself to have sex with him when he wanted. Then he started molesting a young girl in my mother's house. Maybe I wasn't providing him with what he needed and I wasn't getting an education in it. I was still very shy. I didn't want the lights on when we were in bed, and it was not a satisfying form of sex. I learned to look up to him as a guardian rather than a partner.

'I felt very trapped, the more I grew up. But at the beginning, and for the first time in my life, I had a home of my own. He built a little house for us to live in. He was wealthy by now, and I didn't realize what I was missing.

'Then I was being educated to be a teacher. I went on a course in Singapore. By growing up and getting an education, you see other people's relationships. There were no children coming along. My husband was Deputy Minister for Defence in the second year of our marriage. There was no minister above him. He was also Managing Director of the state trading organization. It was more him that helped the President to become the President. He was the Secretary to the President so I was brought into the life of the First Family. So you are a social woman, with certain social responsibilities. I was a beautiful wife. For 16 years, we played this game. Sex was very irregular, if at all and it was obvious what was going on. I would just think: 'He's been elsewhere when he comes home.' I felt we would have to go our separate ways. I remember very vividly six years into our relationship there was a) no sex, b) no children and c) no time together, so the writing was on the wall, but it's not perfectly accepted for a woman to divorce her husband. It's different of course for men. The [islands] have the highest divorce rate in the world. The man just says three times you are no longer my wife, and supplies a written statement to the court. The court tries to intervene nowadays, but not then. Now they fine the man 5,000 *rupiya*. Then there was no need even of a witness.

'About 11 years into our marriage, he was getting more powerful. There were lots of women in his life. As far as society was concerned we were doing allright. I was working full time. My school life was my life. I had brought in a little girl as a surrogate daughter. Then one night I caught him with my maid. I protested and he threatened to bring the police over. My stepmother took me in to her home, then after a week they brought me back to him and again I stayed. It would be disreputable for the woman to leave. His brother-in-law was the President.

'Now he was Minister for Trade, and a full member of Cabinet. There was some financial irregularity, some mismanagement of funds regarding the tuna fishing, and he was told to step down and leave the country. We chartered a plane to England via Colombo, and came here. But I had to leave a lot behind. Because by this time I was President of the Women's Association. I had written a book called *The Spirit of Women*. I became who I became because of who I was married to. I had a talent for being OK with women. People saw in me a leader who could bring in fascinating things for them. I put on concerts, fashion shows, I am a good needlewoman. My role in the community was enormous. There were so many people in my house all the time as a result of this Association.

I did voluntary work to help the community, supporting events. I was a wholly committed voluntary woman, and a very involved member of the school. At 24, I was Assistant Principal of the school, in charge of 2,700 children.

'I put up with the humiliation in the bedroom because of the sense of belonging I got from being part of my husband's family. But I was celibate in this marriage. According to the law, if a man is not bedding the woman and six months go by, you have the right to make a claim. If you prove beyond doubt, the law will allow a divorce. My husband was keeping two other women, besides me – a young girl and the maid. He was keeping them in different homes. He was a workaholic who was released by sex. He was lost to my radar. He would never admit what he'd been doing.'

When her husband lost his job and they fled to the UK, Roxana hoped they now had an opportunity to rebuild their relationship. They would now have some time to spend together. 'I was so wanting to do everything the way he wanted it. But instead, he asked me to bring that woman over. He would phone her early in the box room. Three months later we went home. My sister-in-law did some deal to allow him back home. He was taken to the Corruption Board, but never charged and he was simply reinstated. He was made Minister for Atolls – an even bigger job. He was now the second biggest landowner in the country, getting all these rents. He owns 11 houses, four yachts . . .

'There had been a coup attempt in 1988 when he was Defence Minister. Three guys from Sri Lanka . . . they killed the guard. I told my husband to get out quickly, that I would handle it. And I did. I stood up to them, when they pulled down the door. My husband went into the bedroom. He jumped from the roof and nearly lost his life. He broke his wrist and ankle but got away. He gave me the house after that incident. But it didn't change anything. All these shocks were shaking my resolve to stay. After the Olympics in Barcelona, I decided I had had enough. I met a man

in Barcelona, one of my own people. For the first time in my life
I knew what it was to be loved. He opened something I had never
had before. We dated for three years. But there were so many
layers my husband had worked his way into. He gave me a beautiful home, a family to belong to, and Ayaan, my adopted little
girl who was growing up. It was difficult. I would have been able
to continue all the roles, but without the finance or the material
backing. My teacher's income would not have been enough.'

In 1994, Roxana plucked up the courage and got her husband
to sign a letter of divorce, but it took nine years to finally make
the break, legally and emotionally. She has survived thanks to the
house she owns in her own name – in whose garden she has built
a block of flats which she leases – and by dating various men,
even using a British Asian dating agency – without sex. 'I haven't
allowed them into my life. But you do need to be hugged, to be
held.' Then in June 2005 she proposed to a businessman who had
helped her with the PhD.

'I felt I needed a man who could give me some pleasures but
leave me to run my own life. What I was missing was companionship. I proposed to him and he said, Yes. We needed some time to
get to know each other so we talked, saw each other a couple of
times. He got a divorce. Then I didn't hear from him.' Roxana
learned that this man did not wish to see her again. She was dev-
astated. How could someone be like that?

She muses: 'People are afraid because of who I was married to.'

'I have a yearning for a man. It hits me in the morning. Every
morning I am half-asleep, but I am thinking about one or two
people I love – men I could have had. The conversations go rolling
in my mind. When I come home to an empty house, it's not like
home used to be. I would like it to be like it was with my husband –
children coming up and down the stairs, food on the table, people
looking after me.'

Then unexpectedly, in the same calm level voice, she says she
thinks she needs to see a counsellor before she goes back home to

pick up the threads of her public life. I am shocked – and so is she – to find she is crying. 'I don't know why, but whenever anyone tells me I have done well, I start to cry.' Her tough, poised stance masks another reality that takes her unawares.

Roxana broke open the padded box, the demeaning sham of her marriage and took the brave and unusual step to claim her life back on her own terms, Western-style – but the personal fulfilment of which she dreams is a chimera. There is no social reality in Islam for a woman alone, and the warmth she craves comes at a high price. It makes of abstinence simply an absence; and paradoxically it is guaranteed only in relation to the men who guard you.

She adds: 'I don't know why I cannot find this man.'

Evangelical and single

Conservative evangelical churches have effectively banished their young females to psychological purdah – and their young males strike sometimes bizarre poses, or lead a double life. Such teaching as there is on sex focuses on rules, rather than on love, social skills or the reasons behind the traditional Christian sexual ethic. As 'the world' outside grows increasingly wild and unruly, the Christian Unions ramp up the proscriptions against contact (of any kind) with the opposite sex in what the girls describe as 'the Christian culture' – so sexual exploration has to take place away from it, or when 'drunk', which provides some excuse. Sex is about sin or marriage. Love and romance don't enter into the picture.

I met Lily and Kit at their comfortable digs in Golders Green. An older Christian friend Mark was there – a former Communist Party youth organizer – and he chipped in at the end. Both girls worship at St Helen's, Bishopsgate, a large church in the City of London, famous for boycotting its annual financial contribution to central diocesan funds, over the issue of gay unions. Lily (23) is studying for her Masters at University College London, and had spent time in the summer working for the Church Mission Society at its summer festivals; Kit (24) was a student worker for Agape – the British off-shoot of the American Campus Crusade for Christ. They met at Southampton University, when both were members of the Christian Union.

Petite, with long brown-blonde hair, Kit was poised, steady and easy to talk to. It emerged she had started 'dating' – her word. But this proved to be infinitely more complex a business than I could have imagined. The Christian Union had been the focus of life at university – this was so obvious a fact to the girls, they spoke of it without preamble. For Lily, too, a pretty, outspoken former public schoolgirl, the social scene at university seemed complex and frustrating.

Kit: 'The cool guys called themselves Brothers in Christ. The trendy guys – they didn't make it known, it came out later, but at the end of exams they would fly off to Italy and sleep on the beach and be crazy. They would hang out together and do crazy things to be lads. But they very much weren't allowed to go out with girls, at least not anything serious, and then it all came out one day. This guy called Mike went up on stage with a BIC pen and snapped it in front of a few hundred people. It was symbolic of the Brothers in Christ 'breaking up', he said. Because one guy had started going out with a girl. He had committed treason.

'They created a mystique. Bachelors to the Rapture, you know: "We're going to be single until Jesus comes back." A few are now married though. But it was like, "We don't need girls." The girls then set up a group. But a lot are now married.

Lily: 'If a girl likes a guy, there's nothing you can do. You can't flirt as a Christian. You can be friends and invite them to things. They don't like it if you invite them to things – but then they don't invite you either. But then, when it gets down to it, they don't feel like they have fought for the girl which I think they think is a non-Christian thing. You basically just have to wait for them to do something and they generally don't!

'People talk and think about marriage instead of dating. I have been advised strongly not to go shopping with boys! Love and romance don't come into it. It's such a desperate situation that love comes as a secondary thing! I knew a pretty, normal, Cambridge educated girl and she told me that no one had ever asked her out, or complimented her. One day, she went to her male Christian housemate asking him to tell her what she was like – and he wouldn't. Guys are too afraid even to compliment a woman. Out of 15 boys, if 12 had asked her out, she would have said 'Yes'. It hasn't got anything to do with love and romance. It's just desperation. This is typical Christian culture.

'I think the problem is the guys. There's so many and they think they're great, and it makes girls feel very insecure. It was so sad my friend had to reduce herself like that.'

Mark chips in: 'I think it's men who are the problem. There are fewer men who are Christian. We are less likely to admit our dependence on God and on each other. The level of emotional intelligence of Christian men is probably poor. I just don't think Christian men are addressing the problem.'

Lily: 'We are always being told 'Singleness is a gift' – it's become a catchphrase. It seems to me it generally refers to women! It's hard too, because culturally, a single woman is seen more negatively than a man.'

Kit: 'The family brought me up a Christian, then I rebelled. You would go out and get drunk and pull whoever. When you're drunk, you can take the initiative. You can wear short skirts and say "I was drunk" – which can be your excuse. For Christian men, the only way to express their need of women is the way the world does! It's sex or nothing.

'I've been to a seminar here, a seminar there, but it's never got to the nitty-gritty. UCCF [the Universities and Colleges Christian Fellowship] do a course called 'Pure' on relationships, which I've led. It discusses the roles of men and women after the Fall. We never actually get down to "How do you behave ?" We get a lot of "Don't do this, don't do that and that girls shouldn't wear clothes

that are too tight, too short". Not "How can we have friendships".
And we still don't know how to act towards boys!'
Lily: 'It's all about small rules, not the big picture'.
Mark: 'The cardinal rule of the church just seems to be to respond
by trying to teach rules rather than training in social skills.'
Kit: 'They should teach the reasons for things rather than the rules.
We were taught sex before marriage was wrong, but we didn't
know why.'
Lily: 'I went out with a guy for a year and when he left to go to
Edinburgh I decided to go and see him, and a UCCF worker came
to my house to make sure I wasn't going to stay in his house by
myself. She advised me it would be wrong. The main issue seemed
to be, how it would look to other people.

'Society and Christian culture are so detached from each other.
One of my big problems at university was in the Christian culture,
trying to apply what they teach. A lot of Christian boys will behave
one way around Christians and another by themselves. The Christian culture is a real problem, it's so separate. It's where you don't
admit you struggle with how you play the Christian culture game.
It's then easy to sin because there are such separate worlds.

'The problem is they are trying to teach about dating – which
doesn't exist in the Bible – and basically saying love equates to lust!'
Mark: The church doesn't need to apologise though. I was celibate until I was 44 and never had a problem. I was head of the
Communist Party Youth in Britain until I became a Christian.
My father and mother were Marxists and they were both incredibly promiscuous. When I was 12, my father was arrested, and
I didn't know where my mother was because she was in some
kind of feminist community in Southend, and the local Catholic
family looked after me. I just remember then deciding how much
healthier the nuclear family of my Catholic friends was compared
to my parents' promiscuity. This was the first step in my conversion.
It gave the Holy Spirit so much room.

'When I was 12, I decided I was going to have lots of female
friends and then be sexually active with only one. That's because

my father had five partners and my mother three before I was 12. It was just an unhealthy abyss.'

The young Christian man

Charlie is 26, six-foot tall and a jazz guitarist. A very beautiful youth – one of the most beautiful I've ever met – his beauty is more than skin deep and it affects you powerfully and unconsciously. His face seems translucent, luminous. Blue eyes, a goatee beard and blond dreadlocks in a black alice band. He is slow to speak – an occasional shout of laughter – rather solemn, and his thoughts articulated, as an old wise man might, in the form of Bible texts or doctrinal statements as if they were his own discoveries.

Charlie is a talented young man, a musician in a band, good at hockey and rowing when he was at Durham University. He became a full-time church worker, prior to training at Bible College for missionary service in Japan. Part of his work involved leading sex-education classes for the University and Colleges Christian Fellowship. He lives in a shared house with three males, one a banker, another the landlord who is a 50-year-old chef who attends a famous City church. Charlie guards himself from 'unhelpful' cultural influences, and behaviour that can distract his attention from godliness. He finds the magazine shelves in Smiths 'unhelpful' – and doesn't even own a TV. 'When I did watch TV I'd be watching a load of rubbish that was feeding me a worldly message when I was off-guard, and was not helping me to have godly thoughts'.

His parents were missionaries in Japan, running a guest house there. He had been sent, as mishkids[5] often are, to boarding school, in Cheltenham – where he remained a virgin. He recalls giving his life to Christ aged 7 – after his father suggested it – and he attributes

---

5   Children of missionaries.

his morality to the 'protection' afforded by the Gospel. He also believes his shyness helped, making him unattractive to girls. 'I wasn't that cool.' But the unwritten 'six-inch rule' was an aid to self-control. I hadn't heard of this. He explained (as if it were obvious) that this meant keeping your distance literally by six inches – and definitely no snogging. Pressure to be sexually active increased at university. 'You are considered very weird if you are not.'

He was, he told me, still a virgin 'technically'. He was 'courting'. Marriage was something he was being counselled to consider as a support in mission. He did not kiss his 'young lady' – and they tried to hold hands in a way that did not cause arousal.

Charlie sets a high standard, and monitors himself assiduously, with an almost obsessive degree of self-consciousness, it seemed to me, but also in a way that implied he felt he was accountable for his behaviour to others – people whom he respected and loved. 'I wouldn't say I have always acted with purity and godliness in the romantic relationships I was involved in … Apart from Christ, I am only able in myself to do what's wicked and evil. God graciously kept me. If it was just down to me, I would have fallen in that area quite easily.'

He has known his girlfriend for three years and his courtship, which began in earnest six months previously, seems to have been characterized by utmost selfless considerateness. He has never kissed her. He tries to hold hands with her in the manner of brother and sister, without sensuality.

'When I first met her, I think what attracted me to her was the way being around her inspired me to be a more godly man. Her love for Jesus, her passion for evangelism and her hunger for God's word were attractive and infectious.'

He decided not to 'lead her on' as they were working so closely together, and made no moves so as to cause no problems for her. But she misunderstood, and began dating someone else. He was heartbroken and realized from his reaction just how much he cared for her. After the Old Street tube bomb on 7 July 2005 near where she lived, he phoned to check on her about 13 times but could get no reply. It was an indication to him his feelings for her were serious.

'I was going to stay single for God's work *à la* 1 Corinthians 7, but I began to realize that having a helper and companion could be a great help in the ministry and a great support to me – and as I was talking to these missionaries in Japan I have confirmed that. At the same time I was talking to this girl and talked to my parents as well, and decided that when I got back to England, I would talk to her about how I felt. I had known her for three years by this time. We have been courting since then, continuing to get to know each other and looking towards whether marriage might be best for us.'

One wonders quite how people like Charlie – and I presume there are others – ever do 'clinch it'. But that's the point. For Charlie and his ilk, it doesn't really matter. 'It may be I will stay single – I will know that's what's best for me because God has my best interests at heart, and whether I am married or single, God will give me the strength to do what pleases him.'

He and his girlfriend had both 'struggled' with sex, and had done things they regretted – but they had learned from that. 'The Bible says flee sexual immorality so, rather than thinking how far can we go, or how much can we get away with, to actually think OK let's not go there at all until we are ready to make the commitment for life.'

And if it doesn't work out? – 'There's less mess and regret than if it "worked", and the relationship or the marriage then failed.'

The way Charlie related to his girlfriend is, in the present cultural climate, almost unbelievably circumscribed. 'There are times when we chat on the sofa and I will say I need to sit somewhere else for a while and cool down. Because she understands why I do that, that I am wanting to be pure and we are not wanting to arouse one another, she respects me for that.'

I felt something after walking away from Charlie at the British Library which I feel I have to examine and record carefully, for it was unfamiliar and might prove to be the key to my quest for the meaning of chastity. I felt changed – cleaner, lighter, more hopeful, and certainly less 'cut off'. Was it that his purity, his simplicity, his respect for a girl who set standards he wanted to emulate, had infected me somehow? Was it the unconscious infectiousness of a free spirit not tied to its own ends, agenda or self-gratification? He seemed untrammelled by egotism or controversy, and I felt less burdened after being with him. I wanted to get rid of my own TV, chuck out half my wardrobe, stop worrying about money. I wanted to face the way he was facing, raise my sights, make myself transparent and accountable again. Imagine these feelings infecting the whole society!

Astonished and strangely excited, I got on the bus and went home, as if I had something more to live for. I recalled his saying that what attracted him to his girlfriend was 'the way being around her inspired me to be a more godly man'. I compared that with the sexually aware – 'hot' in the jargon – teenagers in Ariel Levy's masterpiece *Female Chauvinist Pigs* and the one who said: 'I've put so much consciousness into my appearance in the past, now I get scared of having a relationship that's actually based on what's inside of me' – and I wondered what she would give to have a chance to know how inspiring she could be to a good man, precisely for that alone.[6]

The Jesuit priest

It is not easy to interview a famous Jesuit – especially one so imposing as DJ. But he graciously permitted me to ask him anything I wanted – 'Do feel you can talk about the sex and all that', he'd said without prompting. Well, I'd bared my soul to him for

6   Levy, *Female Chauvinist Pigs*, p. 155.

eight days, under his spiritual direction. Now the boot was on the other foot, but I felt self-conscious. This was holy ground. Had we had weeks to walk together over his beloved hills, I may have emerged with different, perhaps more nuanced, impressions. As it was, my questioning seemed somewhat clinical.

He on the other hand had an entirely relaxed acceptance of his own and others' sexuality which he felt should be rightly viewed in the context of relationship. We hardly knew one another, and I felt I was raiding his experience for a task of my own, rather than engaging in a conversation that might deepen our own acquaintance. I trust he will forgive me. What struck me was his total simplicity (what he would call 'poverty'); and the over-mastering centrality of Christ in his life and vision. He made the vow of celibacy seem almost easy, and very normal. Well integrated into a balanced personality, it surely is normal.

DJ went to a Jesuit school in south London. At well over six feet, with a fun-loving, upbeat but gentle personality, he was popular on and off the sportsfield. Rugby was his passion, and when eventually he was ordained, the whole squad turned up, and sat, leaving a gap where the eighth man – himself – should have been.

He was attracted to the Jesuits by their lack of careerism, but has no idea why – and this despite coming from a family of successful doctors, lawyers, financiers: 'Jesuits are just shoved around wherever the need is. I thought, this is interesting.' He signed up at the age of 19 and has remained 'nose to the grindstone' for the last 46 years.

Despite his obvious appeal to women, DJ thought little of what he would be giving up. Girls played their part in his life – but, being the 1950s, he had not been sexually active. 'I could of course, be aroused sexually. But you want to follow Christ and Christ was a celibate. Yes, there were lectures on sexuality, celibacy, availability for the Kingdom, that sort of thing. But it was not, "These are the naughty bits – you must beware them at all costs". Of course, I had the normal temptations. The older I have got, the more central the person of Christ becomes and Christ's relationship with his Father. I am now older than Jesus Christ! It's his giving, serving, being drawn by the love of his Father and wanting to respond that one notices. And his values, I feel, are the right values for the world.

'One side of me would like to be married with children and grandchildren. But it doesn't cause me problems; it doesn't mean I am thinking of jacking in. It's nice to be rung up by my nieces. If I didn't like that, I wouldn't be human. No man is an island and we need other people. My family is important. I know I am loved by them, by friends.'

I put my pen down to listen as he tells me of the searing experience he'd had of falling in love some years before. So overwhelming had it been, he'd considered renouncing his vocation. He had to seek advice. It was Christ, and the reality of a calling to serve him, that proved strong enough in the end to make it possible for him to continue. He does not regret his decision. 'What do people want? They want to be loved. Of course. That wanting to know someone loves them and that I am worthy of love – fine, that's important, it's very liberating'

The experience has helped him to empathize with those he directs who get into difficulties – though he finds that most people who come on retreat are leading 'very good, faithful 'loving' Christian lives'. The 'experimentation' of the 20- and 30-something generation he puts down to 'the geist of the age'.

Marriage is not necessarily the antidote to a failed vow of celibacy. 'Because a man is married does not mean to say he is not going to have problems controlling his sexuality, with masturbation and so on. Marriage, even a happy marriage, is not the way to cope with that side of things totally. And we can also sin against celibacy by being selfish old beggars'.

The eucharist is for him a sacramental substitute for sex. 'It's a very special moment. In marriage, the couple give each other the sacrament through the consummation of their marriage. Sex is part of their relationship, their loving. For me the eucharist – that's God's care, God's presence. That's pure gift.'

Sister Maximilian – Hermit

The solitary – 'a being able to stand at the intersection between the love of God and suffering humanity.'[7]

For former nun Sister Maximilian – as she was then known[8] – it is the union of minds that is erotic, not the sexual side of her marriage. And she does not believe her relationship with God during nearly 20 years in cloister and hermitage were lived as a Bride of Christ either. 'I have never been able to see it as more than a metaphor that I couldn't understand', she says over an apple juice at the National Trust Coffee House in Charlotte Square, Edinburgh, near where she now works as a legal secretary.

'It didn't have any reality to me – when nuns are described as Brides of Christ. I refused to do the Solemn Consecration of Virgins – it's so sexual that service. That's not what I feel. I chose the Monastic Consecration – for when people have been widows etc. I suppose I'm quite a non-sexual being. It just wasn't an issue.'

Magda's parents came to Britain in 1939 from Bratislava, in what is now Slovakia, to escape Hitler's persecutions. Her grandparents died at Auschwitz. Her father, an author and translator, was forced to find work in the travel business. He and his wife ran a travel agency in London's Regent's Street. When she was 25, Magda entered St Cecilia's Abbey on the Isle of Wight, where she stayed for 13 years, before deciding she was being called to the extremely rare life of a hermit.

---

7 Isabel Colegate, A Pelican in the Wilderness: Hermits, Solitaries and Recluses (Harper Collins, 2003).

8 Sister Maximilian's story is sensitively told in Colegate's *A Pelican in the Wilderness*, pp. 232–4, and she agreed to use her real name for this interview. She had taken the name Sister Maximilian in memory of Maximilian Maria Kolbe, a priest who had been sent to Auschwitz for harbouring Jews and who had persuaded the German guards to let him die in the place of a man who had cried out, 'What is to become of my wife and children?'

A slight woman with a sharp almost elfin face, long brown hair and intense blue eyes, she defeats every preconception one might have about nuns. Her quick, short answers foreclose discussion while at the same time seeming to want to provoke further questions. You feel you're being led a dance and, as she says, 'I think in spirals'. But you also get the impression she is trying hard to be frank, to be honest, to be her real self before you and God – knowing full well how mysterious and even contrary both self and God are. It's almost as if she's gently mocking the whole business. Extremely clever, she has degrees in Classics from both Oxford and Cambridge and edited the *Classics of Western Spirituality* series for Paulist Press. Her conversation is littered with references to obscure nineteenth-century divines or continental philosophy. She is slightly fey, shy and childlike and much younger than her 50 years. Perhaps that's what you're like when, as she says, you've 'only been in "the world" about four years'.

She entered the convent when she was 25. 'I had never wanted to do anything else. I was giving my life to God. In my circle, it was considered the best thing a woman could do. Definitely – it was brain-washing. The drip-drip effect, the constant trickle of suggestion. My parents were Roman Catholic – not terribly devout, but they were pro Latin Mass Movement. I was the devout one. It's always been the most important thing in my life – and it still is. He/she [God] still is.

'I heard the call as correctly as I possibly could. For 13 years, I just gritted my teeth. I thought, this is what God wants. I am not very happy, but if it's what God wants . . . I think it's the complete crushing of all personality, and all autonomy. The over-religiousness of things that are not religious. Things are turned into a religious virtue when they're not. Being tidy and so on. Every little detail of your life. The guilt is tremendous. Even so, I would say to someone, if you have to be a nun, be a nun there. It's a lovely place.

'I tried my vocation with the Carthusians for one year. I left them. Then I was leant to a woman who was trying to found a semi-hermitage community. Then I struck out on my own.

I thought you could combine the good things of religious life with having your own relationship with God. I was tired of being treated like a child.'

She seems slightly defiant as she talks, self-conscious, even proud to have been so different – like one who has travelled in exotic places and returned to a world that can barely comprehend where she's been; both loath and keen to share so intense and unique an experience. Yet it had been she who had volunteered the information of her hermitic past to me – by definition so intensely private an occupation – as I stood shaking her hand at the door of the church in which she had just preached. She embodies contradiction.

I had approached her because her sermon had been thoughtful and there seemed something unusually determined in the way she spoke – as if it were coming from some deeper more wrestled-in place of intellectual endeavour than is often the case with clergy sermons. Then I began to understand why.

'I lived in someone's summer house for some time, in Kent. Then a little house on top of a hill. If you have no money it's very difficult to find somewhere to live. Then one wing of a stately home – then finally I lived in a small house in the Borders which I got from a legacy.

'I was there for two years. I sang all seven offices plus two hours of prayer. You can't do that in the world. I tried – God I miss it! But it turns into a chore. I wanted to be myself with God – and as my old abbess put it, if you are actively in the world doing stuff, you can help one or two people, but if you are on your knees praying, you can help the whole world. Yes, I really believe that.'

She says she never felt the stress of solitude. She would rise and say the night office at 4.30 in the morning – and tend a small vegetable patch in between the times of prayer. She supported herself with heraldic art and calligraphy which she would sell to friends – and would emerge from her 'cell' on Sundays to go to

Communion at a church 10 miles away, and to see her spiritual director.

He it was who pointed out to her that she was slowly ceasing to be authentically hermitic. 'I had a friend who was not well, and I was going to see her twice a week. It just went on from there. People seemed to need me more than God did. I stopped being a hermit so gradually it's hard to say when it ended.'

She's now married to her 'best friend' – who is not a Christian. They married in Leith Registry Office. She would still say her 'most important relationship' is with God. 'You are always single with God whether you are married or not. That's what gives my life meaning and gives me my story. But you do put aside a lot of solitude which I miss. But he's worth it.'

A Jewish Catholic Episcopalian. An asexual, married former nun and hermit. A classics scholar married to a lecturer in 'private sector management'. A second-generation Slovakian emigrée Scot. 'I am no longer exclusive', she laughs, somewhat bathetically. It reminded me of something Isabel Colegate writes in her book about solitaries: 'The hermit's calling is anti-institutional. It is also ecumenical.'[9]

Confused? Actually, I wasn't. I was left that evening with a peculiar lightness of heart and a sense of peace and space. Curiously, all those years of prayer and quietness were still infectious. A life lived quite happily in absolute selfless solitude somehow made more room for me. Maybe, as she says, prayer touches us all more deeply and surely than we know. Chastity gives the world a chance.

---

9   Colegate, *A Pelican in the Wilderness*, p. 240.

Chapter 7

Sexuality for Society

> Family breakdown is on a scale, depth and breadth which few of us could have imagined even a decade ago. It is a never-ending carnival of human misery. A ceaseless river of human distress. I am not saying every broken family produces dysfunctional children but I am saying that almost every dysfunctional child is the product of a broken family.
>
> Mr Justice Coleridge[1]

Society's approval of virtue is a key to the viability of the chaste life, for which it will be amply repaid. Chastity has always been political, therefore. From the Vestal Virgins of antiquity through Queen Elizabeth I to Gandhi, sexual continence has been a means to society's strength through the strengthening of the individuals that comprise it. It was in the perpetual chastity of the six vestals – named after Vesta, the supreme guardian of the home and sacred hearth – that the highest authorities of the Roman state and all of civil society entrusted the security of Rome. In return, these revered and powerful women were accorded such exalted status that they alone of all Roman women, enjoyed the same legal rights as men. They could testify in court without taking an oath. For honouring their pledge of three decades of virginity, they were

---

1 Sir Paul Coleridge, High Court Family Judge, in a speech to family lawyers at Resolution (formerly Solicitors' Family Law Association) in Brighton, 5 April 2008.

accorded great respect and many privileges. In guarding the sacred fire of Vesta with embodied devotion, they guaranteed success in battle and the security of the state. Pride in purity and incorrupt-ibility were at the heart of the Roman project. The order survived for centuries. In early Christianity, and for several centuries, according to Carolyn Osiek, 'consecrated female virgins formed a strong characteristic for reasons that have everything to do with the female body as a symbol of political, social, and theological integrity.'[2] Early Christianity actually inverted the honour/shame system of patriarchalism with its theology of the cross, which pro-posed an alternate standard for honourable conduct. Osiek, how-ever, nuances the point by saying that despite this, 'the standards of female chastity and passive virtue were undoubtedly higher than those for male sexual containment.' Nonetheless, the new standard permitted women to be valued without reference to men, as in St Paul's direct naming of women collaborators and friends. It is interesting that by contrast, only one woman is named in the Qur'an – Mary, the mother of Jesus.

Queen Elizabeth chose perpetual chastity for the sake of national unity and integrity. Sir Walter Raleigh named Virginia in America after his queen, whose 'body belonged not to her but to England'. She knew a male consort could undermine her, divide her power, humiliate and harm her. Having been denied their Vir-gin Queen of Heaven at the Reformation, the people of England gained a Virgin Queen on Earth whom they could justifiably revere, alone among women a queen who gave her name to an era.

For men, too, chastity has been the secret of outstanding moral fortitude. success. Gandhi preserved his semen to strengthen his resolve in ridding India of imperial rule. His practice of *brahm-acharya* – traditionally an intense form of sensory starvation in the pursuit of enlightenment – was, in Gandhi's version of it, uniquely Christianized to become a means to social transformation.

---

2   Carolyn Osiek and Margaret Macdonald, *A Woman's Place*, p. 5.

For Gandhi, the end was this-wordly rather than other-worldly. 'His coupling of an elaborate philosophy of militant nonviolence with *brahmacharya* . . . affirmed the power of a celibate lifestyle in the creative process – in this case, the birth of a political movement.'[3] His methods were controversial and would not have impressed the Church Fathers (whom he admired); he deemed it necessary to sleep with nubile young members of his ashram to test his vows. While openly in love with many of them as well as the wife of his youth with whom he later renounced sexual relations, he nonetheless demonstrated a resolve and achievements that indicate the link between chastity and social change for which this book argues.

Chastity and social change

Single women today have much for which to be grateful. Rather than lamenting their lot, like Bridget Jones, they could do more to understand the struggle that has allowed them to remain single in peace and economic viability. Women will always struggle for sexual independence; at present it is taking the form of a disastrous hedonism. In the twelfth century, the death of thousands of Crusaders left Europe teeming with desolate women who seized the new opportunity offered them. In the Low Countries women who lived alone devoted themselves to prayer and good works. Their vulnerability at a time of conspicuous unchastity among the Catholic clergy led Pope Honorius III in 1215 to grant a special dispensation to women to practise Christian charity unmolested, in the hope that their example might spread. These solitaries made their homes on the fringe of the town, where their work lay, attending to the poor, and particularly lepers. About the beginning of the thirteenth century some of them grouped their cabins

---

3   Elizabeth Abbott, *A History of Celibacy*, p. 227.

together, and the community formed the first Beguinage. The Beguine's chastity, and the regard her work earned for her, seems to have been its own protection.

The etymology of the name 'Beguine' is uncertain, deriving perhaps from the old Flemish word *beghen*, in the sense of 'to pray', not 'to beg', for neither of these communities was at any time a mendicant order; maybe from Bega, the patron saint of Nivelles, where, according to one tradition the first Beguinage was established; maybe, again, from Lambert le Bègue, a priest of Liège who died in 1180, after having spent a fortune founding a cloister and church there for the widows and orphans of crusaders.

The Beguine was not a nun; she took no vows, could return to the world and wed if she wanted, and at least in the early days, did not renounce her property. If she were without income, she supported herself by manual labour, or by teaching the children of burghers. During the time of her novitiate she lived with 'the Grand Mistress' of her cloister, but afterwards she had her own dwelling, and, if she could afford it, was attended by her own servants. The same aim in life, kindred pursuits, and community of worship were the ties which bound her to her companions. There was no mother-house, nor common rule, nor common general of the order; every community was complete in itself and fixed its own order of living, though later on many adopted the rule of the Third Order of Saint Francis. These communities were no less varied as to the social status of their members; some of them only admitted aristocrats; others were exclusively reserved for women of humble circumstances; others were completely democratic, and these were the most densely populated. The great Beguinage of Ghent, among several others, became a home to thousands. This semi-monastic institution was well adapted to the spiritual and social needs of the age which produced it; it spread rapidly throughout the Netherlands, and exercised a profound influence on the life of the people. There are still Beguines in Belgium today. Their formation cannot be explained by 'making a go of a bad lot'. Women in large numbers were flocking to the church, following mendicant preachers, joining together to live a life of intentional poverty to counter the new materialism of the age. Poverty and fear were not what drove them; many were noblewomen who renounced property and security; and many were already mothers and not simply evading the terrors of childbirth. 'The new conception of Christianity as a way of life rather than a collection of dogmas, and the understanding that the Gospel's demands were relevant, not only to those ordained by the Church but to everyone including women, inspired many to change their way of life.'[4]

The life of the Spaniard St Teresa of Avila (1515–81) is further evidence of the political significance of chastity. The inner life, considered to be subversive by the Inquisitors compensated for the injustice and irrationality of the external order of things. 'The inquisitors . . . were only too ready to recognize that an interest in the secrets of the inner life was symptomatic of deep discontents with the public order of the Catholic kingdom.'[5] Once again, chastity – a life lived to God – was foundational to new ideas of individual freedom at a time of frightening social tension. The integrity of Teresa's witness made believable her explorations into the radical equality of the Gospel, helping restore for humanity a sense of honour as a gift of God to all people. The taint of subversion by *conversos* – those who had converted from Islam or Judaism for reasons of convenience or status – made everyone's status insecure. St Teresa, herself a Jewess and therefore of dubious status, managed by her disciplined life to reinstate a place for the outsider within the bastions of the church, and despite the strictures of the Inquisition. She showed that honour was not something to be bought or traded but something bestowed by God through friendship with his son Jesus – and all this in the fraught atmosphere of the post-Reconquista. Teresa was as important as

---

4   Saskia Murk-Jansen, *Brides in the Desert* (Darton, Longman and Todd, 1998), p. 23.
5   Rowan Williams, *Teresa of Avila*, p. 26.

the Reformers in her contribution to a modern distinctively Christian European civilization.[6]

The social and economic upheavals of the nineteenth century were catastrophic for women – but it is out of the suffering of women that true emancipation, pioneered by mostly unmarried evangelical campaigners, arose. Women, and not just the new working class who could not rely on husband, father, brother – or convent – for sustenance, had no options. Thousands of female lives were ruined by poverty and predatory men. Single women were assumed to be prostitutes. As such, they could be forcibly picked up off the street by agents of the state under the Contagious Diseases Acts of 1864, 1866 and 1869, and forcibly subjected to painful and humiliating examination by the infamous steel speculum. If they were found to be diseased, they would then be locked up in 'lock hospitals' until cured. For Josephine Butler, who campaigned against the Acts in England, Europe and the colonies especially India, such draconian measures were an outrage legislated and administered by men to provide more *hygienic* sex for men. For Butler, a woman's right to her own body was a legal issue – and that implied the right to be economically viable on her own. Ironically, Bridget Jones scorns her own *enforced* chastity, unaware of the huge price paid by the reformers for women's sexual autonomy, for whom freedom was freedom to avoid sex and sexual interference. When manlessness almost inevitably equated with prostitution, the opportunity to be chaste – sexually independent – was, quite literally, a pious *hope*. To be single *and* economically independent *and* sexually unmolestable was the ultimate target for the pioneer suffragists who hit back at the gross degradation of women everywhere.

Women often rendered themselves – or were rendered – single because their brutal, intolerable marriages forced it on them. If the marriage failed, they were literally outcast, deprived of income,

6 Williams cites especially Deirdre Green's *Gold in the Crucible*, 1989, to make his case.

home, respectability. Singleness required – and requires – the ability to be self-supporting. But work was menial or so poorly paid that prostitution offered a vastly increased wage. Butler's campaigning was against cruel marriages, *and* closed shops. She wrote of the 'two and a half million surplus women' – abandoned or widowed – who were the most vulnerable to sexual exploitation:

> the census [of 1861] does not tell how many of these two and a half millions are working for starvation wages, nor how many of them have declined from a position of respectability to which they were born to one in any class or rank, however low, in which they may have a chance of earning a piece of bread. Nor does the census include among these breadwinners the armies of women, counted by thousands in all our towns and cities, who are forced downwards to the paths of hell, by the pressure from above, through the shutting up of avenues to a livelihood by means of trade monopolies among men, and through the absence of any instruction or apprenticeship to qualify them for employment.[7]

Butler believed that female suffrage would improve this situation, enabling women to fight for their own livelihoods, in an expanded field of possible work. The numbers and extent of prostitution were stunning – especially among the youngest: 'Among the 9,000 women who are pursuing this calling in one of our great seaports, a late inquiry showed that 1,500 were under 15 years of age, and of these about a third were under 13 years of age . . . It is much the same in other towns'.[8]

Butler's campaigning against prostitution was nothing to do with personal vice, and everything to do with male oppression, which both prevented women from entering the trades and professions, and then exploited those it forced into sex work. Much of this

---

7   Josephine Butler, *Woman's Work and Culture*, p. xv.
8   Josephine Butler, *Woman's Work and Culture*, p. xix.

oppression was not necessarily deliberate, she believed. Keeping women out of work, as the inventiveness of the Empire rolled on, was a result, she charitably believed, of

> a transition-period in society; it is in part owing to the rapid advances in discovery, invention, expeditive processes, instruments of production etc., which advances have been unequally yoked with our national conservatism of certain customs, conventions and ideals of life and character . . . Women have been left stranded, so to speak.[9]

What makes Butler's case convincing was her own happy marriage. Hers was a profound and sacrificial altruism. Her homely respectability could not be doubted; there was nothing self-serving in her compassion and indignation, and she was not against marriage per se. The success, the moral force of her campaign depended upon the strength of her marriage – which in turn depended upon the chastity of the *un*married since men were disinclined to marry if sex was otherwise available to them. Chastity was all but impossible for working-class and unsupported women. Loss of virginity through rape, poverty, choice or seduction was the first step on 'the ladder down to prostitution', whether for a maid or a governess. This is reflected in a survey of just under 15,000 prostitutes conducted in 1890 by the chaplain at Millbank prison, G. P. Merrick, which tabulated that over a third were formerly in domestic service. Over half of those interviewed in another survey of 4,000 prostitute patients of the Glasgow Lock Hospital between 1870 and 1880 had worked in factories or domestic service. Friedrich Engels savagely indicted 'the male bourgeois' for female working-class prostitution.[10] Employers seduced servants. Butler's goal was never purity per se but the goal of independence

---

9   Ibid., p. xv.
10   Friedrich Engels, *The Condition*, p. 158, cited by Lisa Severine Nolland, *A Victorian Feminist Christian: Josephine Butler, the Prostitutes and God* (Paternoster, 2004), p. 62ff.

from such sexual tyranny. Indeed, she resigned as World Superintendent of the purity department of the World's Women's Christian Temperance Union in 1897, when she believed that purity as an end in itself had replaced the more crucial goal of fighting the reintroduction of the Contagious Diseases Acts in India. Research by two young Christian women from America uncovered a mass of evidence of young Indian girls being bought, registered, physically examined and maintained in special cantonments in horrifying squalor by the British Raj for use by the British Army stationed there. Butler championed these women, as she had originally done the prostitutes of Liverpool, as if they were her own daughters, despite official denials, cover-ups, public obloquy and threats. She asked: 'What purity could be maintained if the state and the law take it upon themselves to regulate down to the smallest details . . . a disgusting and deadly vice . . . the scourge of the world?'

For Butler, freedom was all. She saw that women could never be free unless they had the vote and could legislate for themselves. She became one of the 1,500 female signatories to the first petition submitted to Parliament in favour of women's suffrage presented by John Stuart Mill on 6 June 1866. She also saw that women could never be free unless they were able to work – and that meant education.

> At the present day women are cheap; their value in the great world's market has sunk to a very low ebb. Their attitude, speaking generally, is that of cringing for a piece of bread. What dignity can there be in the attitude of women in general, and toward men in particular, when marriage is held (and often necessarily so, being the sole means of maintenance) to be the one end of a woman's life, when it is degraded to the level of a feminine profession, when those who are soliciting a place in this profession resemble those flaccid Brazilian creepers which cannot exist without support, and which sprawl out their limp tendrils in every direction to find something – no matter what – to hang upon; when the insipidity or the material necessities of

so many women's lives make them ready to accept almost any man who may offer himself?[11]

Butler agreed to serve as the first President of the North of England Council for Promoting Higher Education for Women. And in 1868 she authored an influential 28-page document *The Education and Employment of Women* which railed against the subjection of all classes of women, especially governesses who were a step above servants, but with no salary, were offered only a comfortable home as 'sufficient reward for accomplishments of the most varied character.'[12] Governesses were especially vulnerable. 'Seldom if ever does one meet with a [prostitute] who is not either a seduced governess or a clergyman's daughter' writes Bracebridge Hemyng in Henry Mayhew's *London Labour and the London Poor* (1861–62).[13] This was partly because knowledge itself was thought to expose women to corruption, and those who taught, however genteel, were therefore already on the first rung of the ladder of prostitution. Butler was therefore challenging the whole structure of society at its very foundation: she resigned as President of NEPHEW believing the primary battle was sexual, in order to focus her energies:

There were many, I believed who would continue the educational work; but comparatively few who would care to go down to the deeper and more hidden work, and to encounter the special difficulties, the disgust and the sorrow which met us there.

Viable singleness for the early suffragists was an essential condition not just for the prevention of prostitution, but for the promotion of the cause. Around one-third of the national leaders of the campaigning Ladies National Association were not just experienced

---

11   Butler, *Woman's Work*, p. xxxiii
12   Butler, *The Education and Employment of Women*, p. 9.
13   Cited in Nolland *A Victorian Feminist Christian*, 2004, p. 62.

feminists, but were unmarried. Butler believed single women were indispensable to social reform. She wrote:

> I cannot believe that it is every woman's duty to marry in this age of the world. There is abundance of work to be done which needs men and women detached from domestic ties; our unmarried women will be the greatest blessing to the community when they cease to be sour by disappointment or driven by destitution to despair.[14]

If women were able – and permitted – to contain their sexuality, not just women but society as a whole would benefit. Sexuality once again became profoundly political. At a difficult time for women and society, '[t]he campaign . . . toughened them against public hostility and ignominy and gave them an infrastructure of political protest.'[15] For Butler, a woman's body was the arbiter of social welfare. Freedom for women and well-being for society entailed both the opportunity for sexual abstinence and the conditions for economic independence. Butler was thoroughly modern in the sense that she believed things could get better. A sense of the body in its social context was a prerequisite of the fight for women's rights.

14   Butler, *Woman's Work*, p. xxxv.
15   Melanie Phillips, *The Ascent of Women*, p. 86.

Chapter 8

Surviving Chastity

Where the assessment, far less the assertion, of right from wrong indicates a moral sensibility, the attempt to live a biblical chastity today may be a form of career suicide. Chastity has always carried with it an implicit reproach. In the thirteenth century, a woman who refused a priest's sexual advances, thereby implicitly criticizing the moral standards of the Church and placing herself above them, was relatively easy to accuse of the anti-procreationist heresies of the Albigensians and Cathars. Some were even martyred for saying 'no'.[1] The contemporary obstacles to reclaiming chastity as a plausible discourse are just as awesome. Yet society itself is at stake. We must re-cast our bodies in terms of charity and community, rather than the distorted secular form of fulfilment that is self-gratification.

The chastity that singleness demands of Christians goes counter to so much around us. It is easier to view it as a 'problem' to be solved, by dating agencies, 'special friendships', different kinds of intimacy, or prayer – which is to fall into the trap secular society lays for us. Our lives are a process, a journey, not an object to be fixed. It is society that has problematized chastity, and the church often follows suit, branding the chaste as merely the choiceless. Society cannot bear the reproach that chastity unarguably is, and

---

1   See Herbert Grundmann, *Religious Movements in the Middle Ages* (University of Notre Dame Press, 1995) (tr), pp. 79–80.

casts it in idioms that neutralize and remove its threat. There is a power struggle in other words, and it gets nasty, especially among some who may call themselves Christian but who see chastity along with slavery and racism as an anachronism.[2] To insist that chastity is a prerequisite of a viable society can be the straw that broke the camel's back for single Christians who have given up on what they have come to see as an outmoded and hopeless requirement and need no added guilt trip. But often they have given up on it too soon, or their commitment to it was conditional on the mate arriving eventually. Conditional chastity is not chastity. It is a waiting game – and we may be betrayed by our own illusions in the end. This is what happened to Catherine von Ruhland, who on finding herself still a virgin at 40, decided the church had failed her, and she was going to unleash her pent-up desire on the first ready male that came along.[3] Sex and grumbling are what destroyed the Israelites.

To suggest that there is some kind of simple panacea for the longing that singleness inevitably entails, would be unhelpful and indeed a lie. Each person must work it out for themselves, and the stringency of God is tempered only by his absolute mercy! Indeed, it cannot be borne, as I believe Freud saw, without one's being committed to some other objective. The conviction that one is part of a great civilizational project is essential. As Alan Bloom writes: 'Civilization or, to say the same thing, education is the taming or domestication of the soul's raw passions – not suppressing or excising them, which would deprive the soul of its energy – but forming and informing them as art.'[4] To be chaste

---

2   Lisa Clark's column in the formerly evangelical *Third Way* magazine, espousing the right of unmarried Christians to lead openly sexual lives, provoked a year-long correspondence. One reader wrote: 'I suspect that most of Lisa's generation will find it as hard to stomach the racism and repression Martin Luther urged, or George Whitefield's use of slaves to build his orphanages, as to understand why sex outside marriage is such a heinous sin. To the guardians of evangelical morals, however, it is, apparently, all very simple.'

3   This story is related in 'An Unchosen Chastity', *Third Way*, Spring 2004, 27:5.

4   Bloom, *The Closing of the American Mind*, p. 71.

is to embrace the fullness of our creativity and of our Christian discipleship, and refocus them. What is essential is a changed perception of oneself and one's meaning – and for that there is no alternative to a daily reckoning with oneself. Chastity is a form of poverty that is foundational to spiritual growth. It is an aridity that cleanses the doors of perception and helps one begin to see God and his purposes. Ambrose describes it as 'a martyrdom'.[5] As St John of the Cross put it, it is a dark night of the soul, requisite to the transformation of possessive love. We begin to look at reality 'in its totality and its wildness'. It is painful and we experience it as desolation, even abandonment. But if we go forward into it armed with faith, and not with the tenets of the world around us, we will start to experience a new reality. Instead of seeking to possess life through love, we will begin to see it more as it exists in itself, in all its complexity and beauty. 'Too many young people', says journalist Kathleen Norris 'grow up understanding that "true love" means possessing and being possessed. This is one of the roots of the huge increase in violence in our cities.' The 'If I can't have her, nobody will' psychology – which she calls a 'consumer model of love'– spurs on at least half the murders in North Dakota. 'They can't allow a former boyfriend or ex-wife to be an independent human being.'[6] The alternative is chastity. Says Rolheiser, 'The gaze of possessiveness, lust, and jealousy turns into the gaze of admiration; possessive consciousness turns to appreciative consciousness.'[7]

It needs to be worked at – and on a daily basis. To be chaste entails being present to God and to the reality of our own hearts at every moment, if we are not to find ourselves out of kilter, listing emotionally to port or starboard as we duck the myriad

---

5 'you are a martyr for Christ when, mindful of the coming judgement of Christ, you maintain a chastity of body and mind in the face of the enticements of sexual promiscuity.' *Exposition of Psalm 118.*
6 Norris, *The Cloister Walk*, p. 259f.
7 Ronald Rolheiser, *The Shattered Lantern*, p. 80.

assaults of the world around us generating false needs and expectations that cannot be satisfied. There is also the danger of emotional deficit – our shadow in Jungian parlance – rising up like a monster in our blind spot, and swallowing us up. This can cause a catastrophic precipitation. We must 'dance with our shadow' in a radical honesty with ourselves and others, risking intimacy, redrawing the boundaries when necessary, recognizing our neediness, and need for forgiveness, learning about our nurture.

It might begin with the *Examen*. The *Examen* is an Ignatian discipline, practised at least once a day, usually in the evening, when one looks back over the day and, in simple terms, tries to understand the moments and sources of consolation and desolation it has brought us; the 'movements' of the spirit, as Ignatius called them. It is a time to give thanks for those things that bring us closer to Christ and the peace he promises (which we cannot manufacture for ourselves), and a time to ask for help to rectify or rebalance those things that do the opposite. I have tried to practise this for many years, and have discovered the truth of Christ's saying that 'Sufficient unto the day is the evil thereof'. Each day is enough of a challenge – and enough of a gift. We will be given enough grace to cope with what is unpleasant in it, and there will always be something for which to be profoundly glad. It is peace on this daily basis that is our birthright, and our joy, not those possessions we feel the world owes us. Sociologist David Martin believes our ability to endure those states whose ultimate consolation is God himself, has been eroded by new forms of religiosity that have usurped the traditional cross-centred life. He calls this 'happy consciousness', a simplified, naive power-and-happiness ideology which leads to a variant of self-gratifying materialism which is not authentic Christianity. 'Power and happiness are very much crucial elements in charismatic Christianity. The older tradition of Christianity understood the terror of judgement and death and redemption. The Crucifixion was at the centre of it, just as it's at the centre of European art.'[8] This ideology destroys the peace that would otherwise make space for others and flow out in renewing energy into the world.

I have tried to avoid over-use of the word 'celibacy' throughout this book, as that implies too long-term a way of living the reality of chastity for most people. It implies, wrongly I believe, a rare vocation, a vowed, often monastic way of life with a different set of intentions and supports. It can also be a cop out for the average singleton! – I for one did not set out to be 'a celibate', but realized eventually that I am. When I became a Christian I discerned a new freedom and sense of self that came from the insight that God himself was in love with me. The overwhelming intuition of that love proved incompatible with sexual relationships. But I still continued to fight the label 'celibate', feeling I should be married and would be eventually; that it was my 'right' and that something was conspiring against nature's best intention for me. Eventually a Catholic sister who taught me much about Ignatian spirituality, said to me, 'You are celibate until you are not!' And that is very helpful. For it changed my orientation. I discovered it was better to live ardently and creatively seeking chastity's meaning, than fitfully seeking a mate with all the attendant frustrations, distractions, and limitations which 'war against the soul.'

If sex outside marriage is essentially harmful to self and diminishes society, which is the case I have sought to make, rather than moving the goalposts we must learn to understand the promise of God in chastity, and ask him daily to show us what he has for us in it. It *is* a daily covenant. Unless chastity is lived in the round, it will feel like a curse. The prayer of consciousness where we see ourselves and our condition as *given for* something else – that charity which is the freedom to be present lovingly to all things

---

8   Conversation with author.

and people – will save us. This insight is a gift of the spirit, and cannot be manufactured. It can be prepared for through orientation and discipline – call it *spiritual hygiene* that creates the right interior atmosphere. Surviving chastity begins – but does not end – with prayer.

Contemplation

Chastity requires a decided turning away from egotistical stresses in life. The moral imperative over the past two centuries on making as much money as possible, with all its attendant activism, renders busyness a status symbol – a perversion of the Calvinist work ethic which saw industriousness and the wealth it generated as a sign of respectability to be invested in the common good. And since respectability entitled you to partake in Holy Communion, busyness became the external sign of your 'election' for salvation. Yet this activism has become an end in itself, a curse, unhinged from any eternal significance; and according to Thomas Merton is the most serious problem facing America and all that America influences.[9]

True contemplation is costly, but it provides the antidote to loneliness and restlessness as Ronald Rolheiser's research has shown. Contemplative prayer, he says, is the route back to that childlike sense of astonishment we once had, a 'revirginization of the soul' which cures restlessness, bitterness and compulsions. It requires single-mindedness, a focus on another reality. Traditional cultures often manifest it. Anyone who has travelled in remote parts of Africa will have encountered it. The ability to live simply in the vast and – to the Westerner, terrifying – empty spaces of the African continent, devoid of material security is an achievement

---

9 Thomas Merton, *Contemplation in a World of Action.* Or as Pope Benedict XVI said at one Angelus: 'Much work often leads to hardness of heart … dedication to silence and contemplation is needed to properly balance our other activities.' *The Tablet,* 2 September 2006.

which communicates itself in the unhurried gentleness of African voices. To live calm and contented without material goods, in the certain knowledge of the inevitability of death requires what the Desert Fathers called *stabilitas*. The ability to stay in one place always, not to succumb to *accidie* or despair, to live contentedly with only the barest essentials of life, this ability both facilitates and is facilitated by chastity. Chastity requires a kind of timelessness; a trust in providence; a joy in the little rather than the much and the many; curiously both a letting go of desire, and a giving in to it.

It is possible, by developing an inner contemplativeness, to become more outwardly attentive; to become less *needing*. This cannot be achieved through striving. It is a loving attentiveness that does not grasp, does not seek after gratification or entertainment; is focused on God and at the same time is alive to creation. It is not self-derived. It is a response to something outside ourselves for which we are created to long. We usually cannot heed it in the noise and hurry, the sheer avariciousness of modern life. It is a calling – literally. We respond in this way because a loving, mysteriously sensed voice imperceptibly draws us. The more we simply open up to it in prayer, the more our restlessness and acquisitiveness and fear abate. It may take a while. But eventually, we learn to unfold. In extolling the benefits of his conversion, St Cyprian included the ability to experience solitude with equanimity. 'Someone who is surrounded by great crowds of supporters and is honored by an entourage of attendants will consider solitude a punishment. As long as we allow ourselves to be trapped by these outward allurements we will be . . . a prey to our lusts.'[10] Lusts appeal to the ego, the need for security, and create more not less need. To find the true source of security and satisfaction, we need outward peace enough to hear what T. S. Eliot calls 'the voice of this calling'. The prayer which leads

---

10 'A Reading from the letter of Cyprian to Donatus' in *Celebrating the Saints*, 2004.

us into a peace that permits gratitude and stills our restless yearnings is not meditative prayer, but contemplative prayer. Rolheiser explains that this kind of prayer is not *about* God, but is *in* God. He uses the analogy of a mother using pictures of water to explain to a baby fish what water is like. The best way to know water is to be in it. Distractions in prayer are usually thought to be counter-productive – and so they are, when meditating on a piece of scripture, or on God's love, or on any particular thing for which we pray. But in the prayer of contemplation, we are free to let our thoughts wander, gently bringing them back to the centre each time we become conscious that we are concentrating too hard on something, even if it's something about God. That centre can be regained by what is described in *The Cloud of Unknowing*[11] as 'a piercing dart of longing love' – reinforced perhaps by a single word, such as 'Father' or 'Jesus'. We won't know whether we're praying at first, and whether it's having any 'effect' for some months. Then, 'we will know by asking ourselves, Am I now more restful than restless; more free than compulsive; more calm than hyper; more patient than impatient; more humble than competi-tive; more self-forgetful than self-preoccupied; and more grateful than bitter?' This is chastity.

Everyone is trying to fill their inner emptiness instead of rec-ognizing it as the gateway to a simpler, more authentically given life. Sebastian Moore explores this in a profound essay, *The Inner Loneliness* in which he suggests what it is that all people long for most: a love that is wholly a 'being-for' one. Part of the problem is that no human can love us in that way; in a way that totally satis-fies. No one can be so 'for us' that they are not 'for themselves' – i.e. other than us; and no one can be so fitted to our own inner dimensions that their 'being-for' us is enough. Moore says it is because what we want is logically impossible. We want a love that

---

11   *The Cloud of Unknowing and Other Works*, translated with an introduction and notes by
        A. C. Spearing, 2001.

we can perceive – because it is 'other than' or 'over against' us. And yet we also want this love to be so totally identified with us, so 'for us', that it mingles and dissolves totally into us; as it were, to *become* us. But that clearly is impossible. We love others precisely because they are other than us: 'We *only* perceive lovingness in definite people who have plenty of interests *other than* ourselves' says Moore. Only God is totally 'for us', and we have to accept that on trust, and on the evidence around us. 'The heavens declare the glory of God', says the psalmist. God has created a world to sustain us, a world for us to enjoy. If God were perceivable in any other way, he would not at the same time be 'being for' us.

Like Rolheiser, Moore writes about another way – an opening of the heart–mind to an inconceivable beauty which is achieved by means of a disciplined 'thinking-about-nothing'. Rolheiser recommends this discipline as an antidote to much of secular living. Secular society, he believes, cannot sustain the demands of faith because it is too narcissistic, pragmatic and restless. Our ability to see God, learned in contemplation, has atrophied like an unused muscle.

> The road back to a lively faith is not a question of finding the right answers, but of living in a certain way, contemplatively . . . God does not enter our world, or our lives, as the conclusion of a mathematical equation or a philosophical syllogism. God enters the world as the conclusion of a gestation process. We must live in such a way that we give birth to God in our lives.[12]

Chastity and the recovery of community

Marriage is no cure for the loneliness that the single person will sometimes suffer. Philip Welsh says it is strange how often married

12   Ronald Rolheiser, *Lantern*, p. 170.

people look back on singleness for its freedom, while singles are trying as hard as they can to give that freedom away. 'Our aloneness may not be something we need to lose, but something we need to find.'[13] We can only live single or married by living unpossessively. Where Anthony Giddens is concerned with 'autonomy' – the ego-driven desire to be beholden to no one – Sebastian Moore is far more ambitious for humanity. He would dismiss Giddens' 'pure relationship' between a man and a woman, or most perfectly for Giddens, a man and a man, negotiating the meeting of needs, as 'mere functional complementarity'. It has nothing to do with wholeness, and guarantees nothing except enduring emptiness.

The antidote to the 'inner loneliness' is not to turn to sexual relief, extreme sensations, drugs or busyness. Neither is it the adoption of a pose, a pious commitment to fulfilment in God alone. 'No conclusion could be more erroneous' says Moore.[14] On the contrary, the effect of experiencing the more radical fulfilment of our desire for being-for (in God) is that one will experience that desire more intensely in relation to other persons. For, experiencing myself as 'special' absolutely and 'for God', for the ultimate mystery, I have a much fuller conviction of my specialness as a gift to others.

This is the key to community. True community is more than the family, the clan, the tribe or the 'in-group'. It is nothing less radical than the Kingdom of God – or, as Moore puts it, 'the polity of God'. 'No God-experience that bypasses the community can be a valid God-experience'.[15] Jesus commanded us *first* to love the Lord with all our strength' *then* to love our neighbour as ourselves – a command which, he said, was *like* the first. '*Until* a person has that fullness of self-love which is only found in being-for

---

13   Philip Welsh, *The Single Person*, p. 5.
14   Sebastian Moore, *The Inner Loneliness*, p. 13.
15   Ibid.

God, he or she is correspondingly restricted in the power to love the neighbor'. Right self-love leads to self-gift. What distinguishes Christian mysticism from all other forms of it – including a romantic escapism from wearisome humanity – is precisely the corporate and communal aspect of the life. This is the love that in the end 'breaks down the dividing wall' by risking the other in a radical openness, a self-giving love that may be rejected or violated – and yet will eventually triumph as Christ did, in resurrection. Even – and especially – the hermit can realize such love. In a paper on the hermitic life given by Roland Walls at a conference in 1977, the founder of the 'skete' Community of the Transfiguration at Roslin in Scotland, said:

> It is the Psalter more than anything else that has . . . prevented [the hermit] from escaping into a life abysmally concerned with soul culture, or losing his identity among undifferentiated contemplatives of all religions. The Psalms are the solitary's prayer book . . . The staple offering of praise, thanksgiving, penitence, and petition takes the same form as that of the universal Church, of Israel, of Christ himself. Alone, but never alone, the hermit joins all suffering, sinful, despairing, as well as happy, humanity in articulating its unsaid prayer.[16]

Christ himself prayed the Psalms. The Psalms strengthen the bond to Christ, and through Christ in prayer, to the world.

Contemplation is genuine openness to and union with others, since it both permits and becomes lovingly aware of, the otherness of others. Contemplation therefore generates community, which in turn nourishes our individuality. 'Individuality is not

---

16 *Solitude and Communion: Papers on the Hermit Life* given at St David's, Wales. A 'skete' – same root as the word 'ascetic' – means a training place for the warfare of the spirit. The earliest sketes were formed in the desert west of the Nile Delta in Egypt, and consisted of four or five men grouped around an abba, or father – one who could guide or counsel.

incompatible with communion but is rather dependent upon it . . . Conversely, lack of community eventually destroys self-identity.'[17] Lack of community also destroys learning and with it, culture. 'The real community of man', says Alan Bloom, 'is the community of those who seek the truth . . . that is, in principle, of all men to the extent they desire to know.'[18] The constraining vulnerability of chastity demands self-knowledge and comradeship, openness and wisdom.

Perhaps uniquely in history, there are new possibilities for the single woman today. A new type of friendship – based on a new type of culture made possible for women by women – emerged in the 1920s and has evolved over time. Friendship among women became acceptable only as a result of the suffragists' movement. Before that, friendship among women was either impossible or immoral – either through constraints of time (it is often still the case) or because it was perceived to threaten family life itself. Virginia Wolf writes:

> 'Chloe liked Olivia,' I read. And then it struck me how immense a change was there. Chloe liked Olivia perhaps for the first time in literature . . . And I tried to remember any case in the course of my reading where two women are represented as friends . . . But almost without exception they are shown in their relation to men.[19]

Nietzsche says that women's friendship had not been possible in the way it was for men, for whom it was based on equality and activity. Elisabeth Moltmann-Wendel makes the striking assertion that

> a cultural change is taking place in which family ties and family norms are fading into the background and being replaced

17   Rolheiser, *Lantern*, p. 56.
18   Alan Bloom, *The Closing of the American Mind*, p. 381.
19   Cited by Elisabeth Moltmann-Wendel, *Rediscovering Friendship*, 2000, p. 1.

by the most diverse kinds of groups of friends, on the same footing as the family or as a substitute for it.[20]

This new kind of family is made possible through the trust engendered in chastity that does not possess or cheat. Hermetically sealed marriages where the wife attempts to control her untrustworthy husband by shutting out friends and family are doomed. On the other hand, open marriages experimented with in the 1960s and 1970s proved chaotic and disastrous particularly for children. But generous marriages that offer themselves in hospitality to others, particularly singles, are the bedrock of healthy communities because they tend over time to afford stability. Economic overmobility is a countervailing force that is both product and producer of pain. Sixty-two per cent of wives surveyed in 1981 said they experienced loneliness as a result of frequent moves. Indeed, loneliness was the most common problem to be reported in a survey of 38 junior hospital doctors and their wives.

> These wives found that mobility was isolating because it both severed established ties with relatives, friends and neighbours and placed them in new and unfamiliar situations. When moves were frequent, feelings of non-belongingness were ongoing . . . building up new relationships was usually a lengthy process.'[21]

Economic overmobility is caused often by the restless pursuit of satisfaction and is a key driver of secularization. Churches, which are sociologically and historically the root of community, depend on stability and their demise is partly accounted for by the 'on-yer-bike' loadsamoney culture. Displacement has become

---

20   Ibid.
21   Faith Elliot Robertson (1981), 'Mobility and the family in hospital medicine', *Health Trends*, 13, 15–16.

a way of life. Blogging, the mobile telephone, ipods are all modern aspects of the attempt to compensate for the subliminal misery of disconnection. Chastity as a proper approach to life sustains community and vice versa.

Chastity demands personal and total commitment. It requires a brave, patient and tenacious decision to go against the social and intellectual tide, to face the double burden of an aloneness that having no partner implies. It must be embraced, not simply tolerated. It entails the proactive – and in our emotionally starving age – prophetic attempt to refound community. Where there are difficulties in finding love and affection, they can be addressed. Chastity is not itself the issue. Chastity clarifies what the real issues are, both in self and in society.

Bibliography of Cited Texts

Abbott, Elizabeth (2000), *A History of Celibacy: From Athena to Elizabeth 1, Leonardo da Vinci, Florence Nightingale, Gandhi & Cher.* New York: Scribner.

Allchin, A. M. (ed.) (1977), *Solitude and Communion: Papers on the Hermit Life given at St David's, Wales in the autumn of 1975,* Oxford: S L G Press.

Aune, Kristin (2002), *Single Women: Challenge to the Church?* Carlisle: Paternoster.

Berger, Peter (1990), *The Sacred Canopy: Elements of a Sociological Theory of Religion.* New York: Doubleday.

Bloom, Alan (1987), *The Closing of the American Mind: How Higher Education has Failed Democracy and Impoverished the Souls of Today's Students.* New York: Simon and Schuster.

Brown, Callum (2000), *The Death of Christian Britain.* London: Routledge.

Brown, Gabrielle (1980), *The New Celibacy.* New York: McGraw Hill.

Brown, Louise (2000), *Sex Slaves: The Trafficking of Women in Asia.* London: Virago.

Brown, Peter (1988), *The Body and Society: Men, Women and Sexual Renunciation in Early Christianity.* New York: Columbia University Press.

Butler, Josephine (1868), *The Education and Employment of Women.* London: Macmillan & Co.

—(ed.) (1869), *Woman's Work and Culture.* London: Macmillan.

Clement of Alexandria (Tr. John Ferguson) (1991), *Stromateis: Books One to Three.* Washington: Catholic University of America Press.

Cline, Sally (1993), *Women, Celibacy and Passion.* London: Little, Brown.

Devlin, Patrick (1968), *The Enforcement of Morals.* Oxford: Oxford University Press.

Dormor, Duncan (2004), *Just Cohabiting: the Church, Sex and Getting Married*. London: Darton, Longman & Todd.

Foucault, Michel (1990), *The History of Sexuality*. London: Penguin.

—(1965) [1961] Tr. Richard Howard. *Madness and Civilisation: A History of Insanity in the Age of Reason*. New York: Pantheon

French, Marilyn (1978), *The Women's Room*. London: Sphere.

Freud, Sigmund (2002) [1908], *Civilized Sexual Morality and Modern Nervous Illness*. London: Penguin.

—(2002) [1929], *Civilization and Its Discontents*. London: Penguin (intr. Leo Bersani).

Giddens, Anthony (2002), *The Transformation of Intimacy: Sexuality, Love and Eroticism in Modern Societies*. Cambridge: Polity.

Greer, Germaine (1971), *The Female Eunuch*. London: Paladin.

—(2000), *The Whole Woman*. London: Anchor.

Levy, Ariel (2005), *Female Chauvinist Pigs*. London: Free Press.

Maslow, Abraham H. (1970), *Human Motivation*. New York: Viking.

Mendenhall, George (1973), *The Tenth Generation: The Origins of the Biblical Tradition*. Baltimore and London: The Johns Hoskins Press.

Merton, Thomas (1971), *Contemplation in a World of Action*. London: Allen & Unwin.

Moltmann-Wendel, Elisabeth (2000), *Rediscovering Friendship*. London: SCM.

Moore, Sebastian (1982), *The Inner Loneliness*. London: Darton, Longman & Todd.

Murk-Jansen, Saskia (1998), *Brides in the Desert*. London: Darton, Longman & Todd.

Nafisi, Azar (2003), *Reading Lolita in Tehran: A Memoir in Books*. London: Fourth Estate.

Norris, Kathleen (1997), *The Cloister Walk* New York: Riverhead.

Osiek, Carolyn and Margaret Y Macdonald (2006) *A Woman's Place: House Churches in Earliest Christianity*. Minneapolis: Fortress Press.

Perkins, Robert (1991), *Into the Great Solitude: An Arctic Journey*. New York: Henry Holt.

Phillips, Melanie (1997), *The Corruption of Liberalism*. London: Centre for Policy Studies.

—(2004), *The Ascent of Woman: A History of the Suffragette Movement and the Ideas Behind It.* London: Abacus.

Pollock, John C. (1958), *Shadows Fall Apart.* London: Hodder & Stoughton.

Reich, Wilhelm, [tr. Theodore P. Wolfe] [1948] (1975), *Listen Little Man!* London: Pelican.

Richardson, Herbert (1973), *Nun, Witch, Playmate: the Americanization of Sex.* New York & Toronto: Edwin Mellen.

Riley, Patrick (2000), *Civilizing Sex: On Sex and the Common Good.* Edinburgh: T&T Clark.

Rolheiser, Ronald (1994), *The Shattered Lantern: Rediscovering the Felt Presence of God.* London: Hodder & Stoughton.

Schluter, Michael (1993), *The R Factor*, London: Hodder.

Scruton, Roger (2006), *Sexual Desire: A Philosophical Investigation.* London: Continuum.

Sipe, Richard A. W. (2004), *Living the Celibate Life: A Search for Models and Meaning.* Chawton: Redemptorist.

Spearing, A. C. (2001), tr. *The Cloud of Unknowing and other works.* London: Penguin.

Thomas, Gordon (1997), *Trespass into Temptation: The Reality of Celibacy in the Church.* Oxford: Lion.

Walby, S., Allen, J. (2004), *Domestic Violence, Sexual Assault and Stalking: Findings from the British Crime Survey.* London: Home Office Research Study.

Walls, Roland (1977), 'The biblical background to the solitary life' in Allchin, A. M., *Solitude and Communion: Papers on the Hermit Life* given at St David's, Wales by Orthodox, Roman and Anglican contributors. Oxford: Fairacres .Publication No 66, pp. 48–53.

Weber, Max (1930), *The Protestant Ethic and the Spirit of Capitalism.* Tr. Talcott Parsons. London: George Allen & Unwin Ltd.

Welsh, Philip (1980), *The Single Person.* Oxford: Fairacres.

Williams, Rowan (1989), *The Body's Grace.* 10th Michael Harding Memorial Address.

—(1991), *Teresa of Avila.* London: Geoffrey Chapman.

Wilson, Philip B. (2005), *Being Single: Insights for Tomorrow's Church.* London: Darton, Longman & Todd.

Index

162   *Index*